Book 1, The Pet Bereavement Series

My Dog Is Dying: What Do I Do?

Emotions, Decisions, and Options for Healing

Wendy Van de Poll, MS, CEOL

DISCLAIMER

If you are ever feeling like you can no longer function with your life, become suicidal, and any of the normal grief feelings have become extreme for you, then that is considered unhealthy grief. This is the time to call your hospital, medical practitioner, psychologist, or other health care provider that is trained to help you. Do not isolate yourself if you are experiencing unhealthy grief. Get the professional help that you require.

THANK YOU!

Thank you for purchasing *My Dog Is Dying: What Do I Do?* As a way of showing my appreciation, I have a gift for you: Your Dog Grief Support Kit that you can use while reading this book.

To Download Your

FREE Dog Grief Support Kit

Please Go To:

https://centerforpetlossgrief.com/book1giftsignuppage

This book is dedicated to Marley, my soul sister dog who died way too early from cancer. Her doggie wisdom taught me that choosing happiness was the right path to take.

Contents

Introduction

You just came home from the veterinarian's office, and it feels like a brick hit you right smack on the head. You heard that your dog has a life-threatening illness. That's right . . . she only has one week or, at best, a few months to live. And to top that off, your veterinarian tells you, "There is no cure."

What are you going to do? She is your best friend and is always there for you, showering you with unconditional love and sloppy kisses.

You are numb beyond belief.

The good news is in this book, I'm offering you tools to support you in your grief and guide you on how to stay present through the muck of caretaking a terminally ill dog. In this book, I supply you with options, so you can begin to heal your pet grief during this special time. I will support you right away in your pet grief journey.

This book is for you if you received news that your dog is going to die, time is limited, and you want to do the best you can to support your dog through this special time during his or her cycle of life.

My Dog Is Dying: What Do I Do? has been designed just for you. It is your emotional emergency first-aid kit that will support you through the rollercoaster ride that you are about to take.

It is your handbook and journal to always keep with you, packed with useful information. Consider it your new best friend.

My Dog Is Dying: What Do I Do? will be there for you always, supporting you as a close friend to walk the journey of pet loss grief with unconditional love.

Something special I'm offering you that I've not found in other pet grief books are contemplation questions. At the end of each chapter, you will find three *Contemplation Questions*, designed to help you proceed even more deeply on your grief journey to become an active participant when coping with your dog's illness.

You see, I myself got the death sentence for my beloved Samoyed Marley, who at the young age of twelve was diagnosed with nasosarcoma. She was given two weeks, and she lived for ten months.

Along with my personal experiences, plus being a certified end-of-life and pet loss grief coach (CEOL), as well as a licensed massage therapist for humans, horses, and hounds, I have helped countless people around the world to never feel alone with pet loss grief again.

People who feel alone with their feelings of grief over the loss of their pets have found support from the suggestions and information in this helpful book.

Denise, whose dog Sadie had cancer, explained—

The best thing about this book is that it can immediately put your mind at ease, center your soul, and provide tips on how to instantly feel less hopeless, less alone, and less freaked out. I use this book everyday to get through all the crazy feelings and situations that come with losing Sadie to a horrifying disease. Plus, Wendy provides an extra bonus of ways to prepare for the end of your dog's life. Without this book, I would be a mess.

I promise you that when you read and follow the tips in this book, you will feel like you have acquired a new best friend that totally gets what you are going through. And I promise it will be your first-aid kit that will give you solutions to some of the most difficult decisions and situations that you will experience.

Please don't be the person who goes through pet loss grief alone. Be the person who actively takes death by the hand. Be the person who can make sound decisions on how to take care of your dog during this special time. And be the person who looks at the pet loss grief journey as an opportunity to not fear death but as a journey to learn, love, and heal.

The book that you are about to read will help you create a compassionate, respectful, healthy, and loving journey for you and your dog to share during this tough, yet special, time.

Remember, you will never have to feel alone with your pet loss grief again!

BEGINNING YOUR JOURNEY: SECTION ONE

Give sorrow words; the grief that does not speak knits up the o-er wrought heart and bids it break.

—William Shakespeare, *Macbeth*

1. Getting the News

Having a dog in your life is so enriching. We all experience this, and we learn a tremendous amount from our dogs. They offer unconditional love that never waivers and teach us amazing things about ourselves if we listen to them.

So, if it happens that you receive news that your dog only has a short period of time to live, then your emotions are probably suddenly creating chaos in your life—you may be feeling extreme anxiety or sadness. You may be unsure of what to do next—how to care for your dog and how to care for yourself.

You may be asking yourself, "Does it ever get easier with my pet loss grief?" The answer—no. However, by understanding what grief is and by employing the other great tools and support offered in this book, you are going to find that you are not alone. You are going to navigate this journey with respect and love, both for your dog and yourself.

You can now consider this book as a new best friend that will guide you and walk the journey of pet loss grief with you. I will help you understand what normal grief is and how you can begin to cope with it in this opening chapter.

If you are feeling hopeless right now because you don't know whom to talk to, how to get help, or whom to get help from—you are experiencing normal grief. This book will help you find support.

If your blood is starting to boil because you are so angry that your best friend is sick and you are feeling guilty, depressed, numb, or even shock—you are experiencing normal pet grief, and the tools in this book will help you.

Once you understand what normal grief is and what the expectations are for yourself, your journey will be different.

Case Study — Denise and Sadie

When Denise got the news that her twelve-year-old golden retriever named Sadie was diagnosed with cancer, she was devastated. When she came to me, it had been three days since the news, and she hadn't slept, eaten, or talked to anyone. She even took sick days from work to be with Sadie because she didn't want to miss a moment with her.

In our first conversation Denise was so distraught, she wasn't even able to form complete sentences when she was explaining the situation to me. She cried hysterically, had bouts of rage mixed with sadness, and at times just couldn't articulate what she was feeling.

Now here is the thing—Denise was having a healthy reaction to the news that Sadie was sick. Denise was experiencing *normal* pet loss grief.

I know that sounds weird, but this is how it works: the fact that Denise could outwardly express herself to someone, who was non-judgmental and could listen to what she had to say without adding advice or suggestions, is what helped Denise understand and cope with her grief, which, in turn, made her grief experience *normal*.

Just to clarify, even though Denise's grief was normal, that didn't mean it was easy or short-lived. Denise was feeling weird about her feelings and not comfortable about what was going on in her mind, in her body, and with her spiritual beliefs. And this is part of the normal, but uncomfortable, grief experience.

Denise had a huge amount of guilt after she got the news. She felt guilty about not doing more for Sadie when she was younger, like the times that Sadie wanted to play ball and Denise wanted to stay inside and work on the computer. Again, feeling such guilt is heart-wrenching but also— normal.

During our conversation, I encouraged Denise to talk about everything that she was feeling and going through—all the feelings that were driving her crazy and how she was going to begin to share this news with others.

The result—Denise began to make sense of the myriad of feelings and physical sensations. She began to understand that what she was going through was very difficult but also— normal.

Plus, she learned that her original expectation—that she could avoid feeling grief—was not realistic. When this expectation changed and she realized that grief was healthy, she felt much better.

Over the course of our working together in my Shoulder to Lean On program, Denise learned that her experiences of pet grief were difficult and uncomfortable but, at the same time, normal, healthy, and special.

By understanding her feelings and accepting those crazy thoughts, sensations, and spiritual upheavals, she began to walk the journey of losing Sadie with respect for herself. This in turn gave her the direction and focus she needed to be present for her dog Sadie and to give back to Sadie the perfect gift—unconditional love.

When our conversation for that day ended, Denise wasn't free of feeling grief. Yet, she had more strength and grounding to move forward to contemplate her next moment in this special journey.

Element 1 — Normal and Necessary

What Denise's story can demonstrate for you is that the first thing about pet grief is to know that what you are feeling and thinking, though uncomfortable and difficult, is also normal and healthy. Grief is necessary, so it is critical that you let your feelings happen.

If you stuff grief down, so many things can happen to your health and well-being. It will affect how you live from the day you receive the news, how you begin to move forward, and how well you are able to be present and supportive to your dog in his or her final days.

In fact, if you stuff your feelings down, your normal grief feelings could become unhealthy grief feelings and actions. We will talk about unhealthy grief later in this chapter.

Normal Grief Feelings — A List

Here are some normal feelings of pet grief that you may be experiencing now or later in your journey.

- *Physical* ~ crying, sobbing, wailing, numbness, dry mouth, nausea, tightness in chest, restlessness, fatigue, sleep disturbance, appetite disturbance, dizziness, fainting, or shortness of breath

- *Intellectual* ~ sense of unreality, inability to concentrate, feeling preoccupied by the loss, hallucinations concerning the loss, a sense that time is passing very slowly, or a desire to rationalize feelings about the loss

- *Emotional* ~ anger, depression, guilt, anxiety, relief, irritability, desire to blame others about the loss, self-doubt, lowered self esteem, feeling overwhelmed, or feeling out of control, hopeless, or helpless

- *Social* ~ feelings of isolation or alienation, feeling rejected by others, or a reluctance to ask for help

- *Spiritual* ~ feeling angry at your deity when a loss occurs or bargaining with your deity to prevent loss

A Life of Its Own

As you can see, normal grief comes in many shapes and sizes. The thing about grief is that it has a life of its own.

What this means is that you can be going through a quiet period of your journey where you are feeling relatively good. Then something happens, and it triggers intense, and perhaps unexpected, feelings of pet grief.

I am here to tell you to let this happen. Let these feelings course though your body. Let them rage. Let your tears flow. It's healthy and necessary.

Abnormal Grief Feelings

Yet, if you are ever feeling like you can no longer function with your life, if you become suicidal and any of the normal grief feelings become extreme, then that is considered unhealthy grief. This is the time to call your hospital, medical practitioner, psychologist, or other health care provider that is trained to help you. Do not isolate yourself if you are experiencing unhealthy grief. Get the professional help that you require.

When your feelings are healthy and you are letting them happen, I can assure you that you will be more present to take care of your dog. You will do amazing things for your dog and yourself (something I'll go into in greater detail in chapter 7).

Element 2 — Reach Out

In addition to recognizing your normal grief feelings, a second essential component for navigating your pet grief journey is to reach out to someone else, as Denise did. Look for someone who will listen to every word of your conversation with respect and compassion, and share your grief experience with this person. In doing this, you will feel better about what you are going through, you will feel supported, and you will come to better understand your own grief.

Element 3 — Time with Your Dog

Spend time with your dog, like Denise did with Sadie. Hug your dog, buy a new toy, talk to him or her and express your love. Your dog will hear you and respond to your love. Your dog doesn't want to be alone during this time as it can be stressful and confusing for him or her as well. Be with your dog and show him or her love.

Element 4 — Familiarize Yourself

Also, get to know your grief. Become a friend to your grief. You are going to be spending a lot of time with your feelings over the next few days, months, and even years.

Spend some time responding to the *Contemplation Questions* at the end of this chapter. These questions will help guide you to recognize your own unique feelings of normal pet grief that you are experiencing.

Chapter Wrap-Up

Having a terminally ill dog is really hard. Your dog is your constant companion. You both love each other unconditionally.

The first twenty-four hours is the time for you to just be in the moment by breathing and preparing yourself for the journey to come. Revisit the four elements I've given you in this chapter and begin to internalize them and act upon them. Respond to the chapter's *Contemplation Questions* to help you manage your normal, but uncomfortable, feelings of grief.

In the next chapter, you will learn how having goals and checklists will help you through this special time. I am also going to share with you the checklist that I give my clients to help in creating your own special list.

Chapter 1 Contemplation Questions

1. What did you do in the first twenty-four hours of getting the news that your dog is terminally ill? How did you take care of yourself and your dog?

2. Now that you know what the feelings of normal grief are, can you list all the feelings of pet grief that you are going through?

3. Are you having any abnormal feelings of grief? Which ones? If so, do you have your health care practitioner's contact information readily available? List the phone number/s here.

2. A Plan

As you already know, it is important for you to be there for your dog right now. Yet, you may be feeling chaotic with the news, and it's hard for you to have positive thoughts.

You may even feel a little helpless about not knowing what is the best thing to do for your dog. Defeat and hopelessness may be setting in, and that can be causing you more stress and grief.

Your emotions are up and down. There are so many things that need to be taken care of, and you don't know where to begin.

A Customized Roadmap

The solution—a checklist. You will design a checklist with your goals and the personality of your dog in mind. The checklist will help you move through your day with your dog with a whole lot more love and a whole lot less chaos.

You will discover that by creating goals and checklists, you will actually stay more focused on your and your dog's needs. It will guide you through your grief to help you stay dedicated to the task at hand.

This is a trying time, and your emotions can zap your energy. Without a checklist you could forget things, be disorganized, and not be prepared for important decisions and events that may pop up.

Creating a checklist that is designed with your goals in mind will help you make decisions, choose veterinarians, and be the best advocate you can for your dog. This checklist will be your roadmap to guide you on how to purposefully live your life now that your dog is sick.

Now, that is not to say that by having a checklist you will not experience grief or that having a plan will make your grief any less important. Instead, a checklist will guide you everyday to stay focused on how to provide the best care for your dog and yourself.

My clients love their lists. They found that their checklists were essential for daily stability. Some even considered their checklists as part of their support teams, which we will talk about more in a later chapter.

Case Study — Martha and Zoey

Martha's dog, Zoey, was dying of cancer, and she was devastated. When she called me, she had just gotten the news the day before and was so confused about what to do.

Because Martha was so distraught, I had her make her checklist right away on our first call. I had her make her own checklist of every task that she could think of that needed to be done.

I then had her make copies of her list and post them everywhere she could conveniently access them. Every morning when she got up, she would look at her checklist for the day and circle those things that she wanted to accomplish.

I explained to her that her list was available whenever she needed support. She could look at it when she was feeling grief, when she wanted to clear her mind, or when she wanted to give Zoey her total attention.

Martha's list was amazing. She had so many wonderful things on it—activities that she wanted to do with Zoey, self-care for herself, weekly and monthly visits or calls to her veterinarian, medication times, feeding times, play times, and everything else that she wanted to accomplish.

Yet, Martha was really tough on herself. She wanted to get things done yesterday. This was part of her normal pet grief.

When she remembered to pace herself with the goals that she'd set out to do and when she remembered that she didn't have to do them all in one afternoon, she created less chaos in her daily life. She was then able to spend more quality time with Zoey.

Martha loved her checklist. It helped her stay focused on how she was going to live her life while taking care of Zoey. Her list provided her with a less chaotic mind and a sense of relief that she wouldn't forget something important.

After Zoey reached the end of her life, Martha revealed to me—

Getting all my tasks out of my mind and on paper gave me such inner peace that when my grief was in full force, I could look at my list, do a task, and then give my dog a huge hug. My list was a lifesaver during my last few months with Zoey.

The List

As with Martha, I have my clients create a main list of everything they want to include as soon as they can. In my Hand to Hold and Shoulder to Lean On programs, we do this very early on.

To make your list, use the *Contemplation Questions* at the end of this chapter to identify the particular activities that you want to do for your dog and yourself; that way you can name the items that are personal to your circumstances and your dog's needs. Once you've created this customized list, you can then download the more general "master list" that I've created. You can download that list at the beginning of the book. This is Your Dog Grief Support Kit, which includes other gifts as well to be used throughout this book.

After you make your own list, take a look at the master list that I created for you. Feel free to then combine the two lists into a single customized roadmap checklist that reflects the plans and needs of you and your dog in your unique pet loss grief journey.

Once you've made your long and full roadmap checklist, you can then draw from it to make daily to-do lists, delineating what you want to do for yourself and your dog on a daily basis. This way, you can keep your long-term plans in mind (via the full roadmap checklist) as you plan out each day. And with a daily checklist of plans, even when unexpected waves of grief hit you, you have a plan to give you the presence of mind to care for yourself and your dog.

This might sound tedious, but remember the goal of these lists will help you stay focused. Have a copy of your roadmap checklist always available as a reference, so every day you can choose those activities that you want to do.

Many of my clients do weekly, rather than daily, lists, so they can plan ahead (an example is included in Your Dog Grief Support Kit). Yet on some days, everyone finds value in creating daily lists because it allows them to be more detailed.

Here is an example of a day in Martha's checklist. She didn't feel it was necessary to include times. Even though there is an order to this list and you see duplicate activities, Martha didn't feel that it was always necessary to follow the exact order. Martha's daily list helped her stay focused and helped her to remember to take care of herself.

One of Martha's Daily Lists

Eat Breakfast

Feed Zoey

Give Zoey medication

Walk Zoey

Do email

Call holistic vet

Snuggle on the couch with Zoey

Research holistic care for Zoey

Schedule massage for me

Cook dinner for both "Z" and me

Give Zoey medication

Play outside with Zoey

Read

Meditate

Give Zoey medication

Bed

As with all my clients, I encourage you to make photocopies of your list and post the copies in various places—the refrigerator, the computer, the bathroom mirror—anywhere that you'll be able to see it frequently throughout your day.

It's important to know that these lists can and will change as your days progress with your dog.

You will probably add new things weekly, maybe even daily, to your list. Consider your checklist to be a really good friend guiding you through this journey. Lists are great ways to stay focused on the task at hand.

Some Dos and Don'ts

Sometimes people will experience their pet grief by feeling like they have to do everything on their lists perfectly and everyday. This is how Martha felt initially. And just as Martha learned, you may also learn that even though that is a normal feeling when experiencing grief, it is important to pace yourself.

It's important to remember that even though you have a checklist, you must spend quality time with your dog. You want everyday to count and matter.

You want to remember every single moment that you have with your dog. You want to create a time where your dog is super comfortable and taken care of.

Without a checklist, the distractions that you have in your everyday life can take over. Then at the end of the day, you realize you didn't spend the time that you wanted with your dog or you forgot something important. Then you feel guilty, which then creates more stress and chaos in your life.

Making your checklist and setting daily goals for yourself will provide you with a way to navigate through, around, and amidst stress and chaos. Your checklist allows you to do things that matter most quickly. You will be able to visit the park, take long car rides, go to the beach, or just lie on the couch snuggling with your buddy because you included these things on your list.

The checklist is a great tool for helping you cope with your pet loss. It will help you stay focused on your dog rather than the mind clutter, which can lead to anxiety. This mind clutter will take you away from living the final days, weeks, or months that your dog has left to live.

Please use the three *Contemplation Questions* at the end of the chapter in conjunction with the general "master list" that you can find in Your Dog Grief Support Kit to create your customized roadmap checklist.

Chapter Wrap-Up

In this chapter, I helped you understand that your unique checklist is a great tool for helping you cope with pet grief. It helps you stay focused on your dog's needs, as well as your own, rather than allowing your mind clutter to take over, which can then lead to anxiety and chaos.

In chapter 3 I am going to teach you about the seven stages of grief when coping with pet loss. With each of these stages, I am going to give you examples of what you can expect from people. Plus I'll teach you how to heal yourself in this journey so that you are ready to deal with whatever comes your way.

Chapter Two Contemplation Questions

1. What are your goals for this special time? Include any new activities that involve you and your dog, and you alone—feeding schedule, exercise times, self-care, care for your dog, veterinarian visits, and anything else that you can think of.

2. Along with the checklist that I provided you in Your Dog Grief Support Kit and the list you made above, can you create your own checklist that includes your unique goals?

3. What are the things that you would like to include on your list that reflect the personality of your dog?

3. Grief and Loss Stages

If you are feeling a little raw with your emotions of grief, that is okay and normal. As I've already shared with you, grief has a life of its own. Know that what you are going through is normal. Your sadness, anxiety, confusion, and anger are okay and healthy to feel. Yet, there is more to your journey of coping with the fact that your dog is terminally ill.

Pet loss grief actually has seven identifiable stages. By understanding these seven stages of pet loss grief, your confusion and possible terror about what you and your dog are experiencing can change for the better. Learning which stage of pet loss grief you are experiencing is extremely helpful to your coping and healing journey. You can gain compassion and respect for your own unique journey, both of which are vital.

Living with a dog that has been diagnosed with a life-threatening illness can be a journey in its own right. Your daily life of caring for your dog that has been diagnosed with a life-threatening illness will change from moment to moment. You want to do the best you can for your loving companion and for yourself.

No matter what you are experiencing while you are caring for your dog, one of the most important things to remember is to cherish the life you are having with him or her right now!

And that includes understanding the stage of grief that you are in.

The grief that you are feeling is a given. It is there, and it's not going to go away. Yet, it will change as time progresses. You will become more and more involved with creating the best life you possibly can for your dog. Your focus will be on your dog.

The Seven Stages of Grief

It is extremely helpful to know not only what normal grief is but also what the normal stages of grief are.

Dr. Elisabeth Kubler-Ross was a pioneer in the hospice movement. While she wasn't a pet grief person, what she discovered can be applied to the journey of pet grief.

In 1969, she made well-known in her book *On Death and Dying* the five steps of grief and/or death. These five steps cover the stages of grieving for the death of a loved one.

1. Denial
2. Anger
3. Bargaining
4. Depression
5. Acceptance

These five stages became very popular and are used widely mostly during the dying process. However, people working in this field began to expand on her various philosophies and standards. Currently there are seven stages of grief.

These are the seven stages of grief that I use in my practice when helping people like you explore their grief and loss stages of pet loss.

These stages will guide you to a deeper understanding of what you are experiencing with your feelings.

1. Shock and Denial

2. Pain and Guilt

3. Anger and Bargaining

4. Depression, Reflection, and Loneliness

5. Adjustment to Life

6. Your New Normal

7. Acceptance and Hope

Over and over my clients tell me that knowing this valuable information now rather than later prepares them even more fully for the future.

Keep in mind that since your journey is your journey, you may not experience all of these stages as your daily pet loss progresses. Yet you may. Whatever you experience is normal, so be compassionate with yourself for what you are going through. Never compare yourself to someone else's experience.

Case Study — Suzanne, Ralphie, and the Seven Stages

Suzanne, a client of mine, experienced all seven stages of grief and in the exact order. When she received news that her dog, Ralphie, had cancer, she called me. She was shocked beyond belief.

Stage One: Shock and Denial

As we worked together, she began to deny the prognosis and believed that it was really not happening to Ralphie. Her dog didn't have cancer, and there must have been a mistake. She kept saying, "I don't believe it, and I am getting another opinion. This is not happening to Ralphie."

Stage Two: Pain and Guilt

She was feeling intense pain. She hurt and was not sure how she really felt at this time. I assured her that this was normal and the second stage of grief.

When the news started to settle in and became more of a reality, her guilt took off like a raging fire. She went through it all. She felt as if she should have done something differently when Ralphie was younger—different food, different treats. She even felt like she could have caused the cancer.

Stage Three: Anger and Bargaining

Then she got really angry at herself and at the disease. She began to bargain and ask her higher power to give her a sign on how she could cure the cancer.

She was so angry that this horrifying disease was killing Ralphie. She wanted it gone, to go away and never return again. She started to hate herself because she believed she caused the cancer. She felt full responsibility, and her anger was immense.

She was so angry that one day she got in her car, went out on the road with hardly any traffic, and then began to yell at the top of her lungs about how upset she was. On her way home

Suzanne told her higher powers that if they would cure Ralphie's cancer, she would never miss a walk with him again and only feed him the best food there was.

Stage Four: Depression, Reflection, and Loneliness

When Suzanne began to understand that anger and bargaining were part of the journey, she then began to feel depressed and lonely.

Her days were filled with intense crying, numbness, and overwhelming feelings of depression. She told me, "I have no one in my family that understands how important Ralphie is to me." Every day she felt like she was totally alone and isolated within her grief.

As we continued to work together, Suzanne began to see her feelings of depression and loneliness were part of the process. Soon she was able to reflect on the awesome life that she still had with Ralphie.

She said to me, "I am so glad I gave myself permission to not be afraid of my sadness and loneliness. Once I understood this part of me, I could again experience the loving feelings that I share with Ralphie."

Stage Five: Adjustment to Life

It was very difficult for Suzanne to transition out of the previous stage and to stage five. She really didn't want her life to change with Ralphie. She wanted everything to be the same.

She confided one day, "Geez, Wendy, I have felt shock, denial, pain, guilt, anger, depression, and loneliness. I have even been crazy angry at my higher power and tried to bargain with them to help Ralphie. Now, how do I adjust to a change I don't want?"

This was a great question. Throughout this book, we will be talking about adjustment to a new life in more detail. Yet for now, keep in mind that this period is about integrating these changes into your daily life to make it work for you and your dog.

Remember Your Dog Grief Support Kit that I introduced to you in chapter 2? All the materials in that kit will help you adjust to a new life too.

Stage Six: Your New Normal

As time moved on, Suzanne began to adjust to the changes and instead of taking long walks with Ralphie, she took him for car rides that they both loved. Suzanne adjusted to the myriad of changes in her new lifestyle with Ralphie, her beloved companion.

She even discovered a group of new friends in the same situation that she was in with Ralphie. Every week Suzanne and her new friends got together at a park, the beach, or somewhere in nature. They brought their dogs and together they shared stories, heartache, and joy.

Stage Seven: Acceptance and Hope

When Suzanne began to experience the last stage of pet grief, she was ready to move forward with an entirely different attitude. She accepted the fact that Ralphie was going to die.

She had found her new normal and had her plan of action on how she was going to take care of Ralphie—what food, what doctors, what new activities. Now she could live every day with him with the hope and desire to do the best she could with the care that he needed.

This was the stage when she became more aware and accepted her grief stages. She was confident that she could provide everything that he needed. It was easier to make decisions through whatever stage of grief she was experiencing.

Chapter Wrap-Up

These stages are references to guide you on how you can process your pet loss. Suzanne experienced all the stages in the exact order. By no means do you need to experience them all or go in the exact order like Suzanne did.

Use the three *Contemplative Questions* at the end of this chapter to help guide you with your unique stages of grief.

Again, please remember that you are not alone with your grief journey. There are others that are experiencing the same thing as you.

In the next chapter I am going to teach you about the myths that surround pet grief and how these myths can hold you back from having a healthy relationship with your dog. I am also going to show you how you can turn these myths around so that they can help you with your journey.

Chapter Three Contemplation Questions

1. What stage of grief are you in right now?

2. How many stages of grief have you experienced and what have you learned about your unique journey through each of these stages?

3. Wendy helps her clients know and understand the seven stages of pet grief early in their journeys. Her clients find that by knowing this valuable information early on, rather than later, they are better prepared for the future. In what ways does knowing this information now help you prepare for your future?

4. Confronting the Myths

Now that you have an understanding of what constitutes normal grief (chapter 1) and have explored the seven stages of grief (chapter 3), we are now going to visit the multitude of myths that come along with pet grief. To introduce the myths, let's return to Denise, whom I supported in her grief journey with Sadie.

Myth Confrontation

My client Denise, on our second call, started to laugh and giggle to me about a situation at work when one of her coworkers told her, "Sadie is only a dog . . . . You can get another."

First she was crying about it, and then she started to laugh. Then she became horrified that she was laughing. She told me that she realized it was really wrong of her to feel any joy during this time of Sadie's sickness and pain.

My response—"Denise, that's just a grief myth. Don't you believe it. You are going to live out the variety of emotions that you are going to feel on your grief journey."

With my guidance, Denise did not stuff her emotions down. She allowed the laughter and the tears to come. In doing so, she really felt relief. She was able to breathe and understand that laughing was another way to express her grief. She felt like a heavy weight was lifted from her heart.

In debunking the "no joy during grieving" myth, Denise finished her session feeling a lot stronger on her journey. She had renewed confidence that she could be the best caretaker for Sadie with more clarity and understanding.

Myths about grieving, like the one Denise voiced, have been around for a long time, and they can either really help you with your grief or be a hindrance to your healing process. The key to making these myths help you is to be aware of them and debunk them.

The Myths

1. It is selfish and extravagant to mourn and grieve the death of a dog when our world has so much human suffering

Debunking—You are a dog lover, and you understand how important your dog is to you. The grief surrounding the fact that your dog has a terminal illness is significant.

People are capable of simultaneously grieving both animals and humans. One doesn't have to detract from the other. By grieving and mourning your dog, you are showing tremendous compassion for the world at large.

2. You must follow the seven stages of grief in exact order so that you can truly heal your pain.

Debunking—Grief is not about following a prescribed list. Grief is tenacious and can really dig in to your daily routine, which can render you feeling hopeless.

The last thing that you need to be worried about is following the seven stages of grief in exact order. Although the stages of grief are extremely valuable, the order in which you do them is up to you. Let the stages unfold naturally.

3. *There is a right and wrong way to grieve.*

Debunking—As with following the seven stages of grief in chronological order, the same is true about your unique grief experience.

Your relationship with your pet is special. No two people grieve the same way. While one person may feel sadness, another person may feel anger about the news. Your grief journey is yours and very unique.

Grieving is very personal and individual to your experiences with your dog. It depends on your personality, the personality of your dog, the nature of his or her illness, and your coping style.

4. *The best thing to do is to grieve and mourn alone, especially because it is just a dog.*

Debunking—We have been taught that in order to be strong and independent we should not share our grief. It would burden and be inappropriate to let other people know how we are feeling.

Yet, it is important to reach out to others. You will want to protect yourself from being judged for loving and taking care of your dog.

Take your time with choosing whom you can turn to for support because some people don't understand or take pet loss seriously. Find a support group, pet loss coach, and/or friend that will allow you to talk about your grief without making you feel crazy or weird. We cover this more in chapter 9.

Yet, remember if there ever comes a time when you can no longer function in life, please see the appropriate health care provider.

5. You have to be "strong" with your grief.

Debunking—In general our society teaches that grief feelings can be a sign of weakness especially in regards to having a dog that is terminally ill.

Feeling sad, frightened, lonely, or depressed are all normal reactions. Crying doesn't mean that you are weak.

Let yourself feel those emotions, physical sensations, and spiritual challenges that you are going through. There is a reason for you to have these feelings. Plus there is no reason why you need to feel that you have to "protect" your family or friends by being strong.

Showing your feelings will help you and may even help them.

6. Grief will go away someday.

Debunking—Never! And that is okay. Our grief changes as each day goes by. You will never forget your dog. Yet your feelings of grief will change.

Never feel like you have to rush through your grief journey. It takes time. Patience comes in handy when you are in the beginning stages of grief.

Your goal for healing your pet loss is not to "get over it." We never stop feeling grief for losing a pet. But we learn to move forward in life again with fond memories.

7. No one gets my pet grief, and I am alone with what I am going through.

Debunking—You are never alone with the grief that you are going through. It may feel like that at times because many people don't know what it feels like to get the news that their dog is going to die. They just don't understand what you are going through.

People (even dog lovers) will say unsupportive things, like "There are so many dogs that need homes. See this as an opportunity!" or "At least, it wasn't a child."

Even still, there are many, many people who do know the grief you are experiencing. It just may take some time to find the right people in your life to support you in a healthy way. There are supportive friends, end-of-life and grief coaches, and pet loss support groups to walk the journey with you. We will talk about this more in chapter 9.

Remember—you are not alone with your pet loss grief.

8. Pet loss grief will go away.

Debunking—Many of my clients call me when they have just gotten the news that their pet is going to die. They feel a tremendous amount of grief and just want it to go away.

It takes work to heal your pet loss grief. Feel comfortable by taking your time. Be an active participant so that you can experience the stages of grief.

Your dog is really special to you. It is really important to let your emotions happen and experience them. If you feel like they will go away on their own, you are only stuffing them in.

And as many of my clients say, "Grief has a great talent of surprising you when you least expect it." So it is better to actively acknowledge, process, and experience it than to stuff it down only for it to pop up in surprising, very unwelcoming times and forms.

9. Once I do all the grief work, it will go away.

Debunking—Once you do all the work in your grieving process, remember that grief can come up again. It is not uncommon to have deep feelings of grief show up again, even years later. It is normal for this to happen.

Grief never goes away, and that is okay. Many of my clients report that when their grief shows up after a few months or years, they are happy about it because it gives them a chance to say, "I love you," to their dogs that died.

For now, since you just got the news, just tuck this thought in a special place, so you know what to expect later.

10. Having a feeling of joy at moments in your life when your dog is terminally ill is not good.

Debunking—Here is the thing—you just got devastating news that your beloved companion is going to die. He or she is sick, and maybe the vet told you that he or she has one week to live.

The last thing that you probably think you are allowed to feel is joyful or happy. In fact, you probably are feeling many emotions from this news, and that is okay.

But it is also okay to experience moments of joy, even when you are grieving about your dog's illness. It is healthy and doesn't mean you are forgetting your dog's situation.

This is a normal response. It is your body giving you a breather from the stress, pain, anxiety, etc. It is a survival mechanism.

11. It is horrible to feel happy or relieved that your dog died.

Debunking—You may feel that it is a little early to talk about this myth, but I believe that it is important for you to be prepared for it now.

Being prepared will remind you when the time has come when your dog has reached the end of his or her life, that it is okay to feel relief and even slightly glad.

This is a very common feeling for my clients that suffered the pain and angst of losing their dogs to terminal illnesses. When your dog is in pain and suffering every day, it can take a lot out of you emotionally, physically, and spiritually. It breaks your heart and can leave you feeling hopeless and helpless.

At your dog's death, feeling slightly glad, relieved, or even ashamed is also a very normal feeling of grief. Keep in mind that it is not a selfish feeling but a feeling that your dog is no longer suffering in the physical world.

The Other Side of the Myths: Grace and Compassion

These myths are very common, and many people think they are true. These myths, in conjunction with the inappropriate comments that people make (more on these in chapter 5) can easily trigger your grief. If you are not aware of them, you could become confused as to why suddenly you are feeling sad or very angry.

Even though they may be well-meaning friends, family, or coworkers, when one of them offers you a myth as a so-called "word of wisdom," it can pack a powerful punch to trigger your pet loss grief. However, once you become aware of these myths and why they are not true, you will be able to react to them with grace and compassion for yourself and your beloved companion.

Here is the thing about believing these myths and letting them affect you—I have seen in my practice that when folks believe and live by these myths, they get stuck with their grief and have a difficult time gaining personal calmness.

When they learn to take these myths, debunk them, and replace them with positive thoughts and actions, they are able to spend more time loving their dogs, rather than being stressed-out with unknown anxiety or other feelings of grief that they may be experiencing.

Please revisit these myths and the debunking of them. They will help you be prepared for the multitude of thoughts and feelings that you will have and the comments people will make.

Use the three *Contemplative Questions* at the end of this chapter to help you to identify and then change any myths that you may encounter in your journey.

Plus, with Your Dog Grief Support Kit in chapter 2 that you downloaded, you can stay aware of the common myths and the easy debunking of them. Feel free to print out the list of common myths and put it on the bathroom mirror, your desk, and refrigerator. Post this list anywhere so that it is readily available when you want to revisit it.

Chapter Wrap-Up

Myths about pet loss grief can be roadblocks to moving forward with meaning and purpose in regard to the bond you have with your pet.

The way to remove the roadblock and make the myths work for you is to be aware of them, debunk them, and then find something positive in them.

To repeat, always remember—you are not alone with your grief journey. There are others that are experiencing the same thing as you.

In chapter 5 I am going to help you prepare for the insensitive things that people will say to you and how these statements can trigger your grief unexpectedly. I am also going to show you how to be aware of these statements before they happen, so you can prepare yourself and won't be totally thrown if you encounter them.

Chapter Four Contemplation Questions

1. Which of the ten myths are you currently experiencing while coping with your dog's illness?

2. Now that you understand what the myths surrounding pet loss grief are, can you add some other myths that you may be experiencing? Can you debunk them and pull something positive out of them?

3. Take each of the ten myths that you relate to and rewrite them to show the positive. Post them so that you can see them everyday.

5. Say What?

When a coworker, a stranger you meet at the grocery store, or even your best friend tries to reassure you by commenting, "It's only a dog . . . . You can always get another!" you may find that your blood suddenly begins to boil and your life in that moment changes. You start to feel uncomfortable, yet you don't know what to do. Should you just smile and say, "Thank you," or should you just politely turn away and go about your business?

I am so glad we are having this conversation right now because first I want to share with you—this is normal. It is normal for people to say things that they think are helpful and well-meaning, but to you are very unsupportive about your dog's illness and upcoming passing. And it is also normal for you to have the reactions that you are having.

What is happening when people say these unintentionally unsupportive things is that they inadvertently fuel and activate your grief. You become sad, depressed, angry, or confused, and you are not sure why all of a sudden you are feeling this way. You likely become confused as to how to handle these people and even wonder if you should continue being friends.

Let me repeat—it is normal for people to say unsupportive, yet what they think are well-meaning, things to someone who has a dog that is ill. And it is also normal for you to have the reactions that you are having.

Now here is the thing—as a society we have gotten very distant from the dying process. We view it as something to be afraid of, and we may even want to avoid it. As people, the more we accept that and allow our grief to happen in a safe environment, then the healthier this process will be.

Remember—your reaction to this person's statement is normal.

I am going to teach you how you can use what you've learned about grief itself (from chapter 1) and the stages of grief (from chapter 3), so you can handle the situation with compassion and grace. That's what we'll be addressing in this chapter.

Case Study — Elizabeth and Emma

Elizabeth, whose dog Emma had cancer, told me in one of our Shoulder to Lean On sessions that after she'd told her best friend about Emma, this person started to avoid her.

Elizabeth was confused and felt very alone. She explained, "My dog just got diagnosed with cancer, and I felt helpless and hopeless. All I wanted was my best friend, someone to talk to, but she is now avoiding me and my dog, and has said some really hurtful things."

You can expect this to happen to you. Because, as with Elizabeth's experience, people dread death, and some will avoid dealing with it—no matter what. As a society we aren't versed in how to go about supporting each other in a healthy way when someone is experiencing grief of any kind.

When Elizabeth became aware of the unsupportive things people were saying and prepared herself on how she was going to react, she found that her support team suddenly grew.

Your Preparation

Right now I want to share with you how you can be prepared for the hurtful things that people will say to you.

I promise you are going to hear them every day, not from everyone, but you will hear them from people that you thought understood what you are going through—just like what happened with Elizabeth.

This is a huge part of your journey when dealing with your dog's life-threatening illness. Be ready, be prepared, and take control of these situations, so you know what you are feeling is okay and normal.

Here are a few of the many things people typically say that my clients have experienced. (At the end of this chapter you will have the opportunity to list some of your own.)

Things That People Say—A List

1. It's only a dog . . . . You can get another.

As a pet parent, you know that the relationship that you have with your dog is unique to the both of you. No one else has that unique relationship as you do.

When someone says to you, "It's only a dog, and you can get another," this is the time for you to respond, "Thank you," and make your exit. To engage and try to educate this person only takes time away from your dog during this special time, which is the place to exert your emotional and physical energies.

2. I am so sorry to hear that.

This one is a big one and the most popular thing to say when we get the news that someone's dog is sick. The fact is that it is not that person's fault that your dog is sick.

I know it may be a moot point, but a kinder, more supportive and compassionate way to respond to this type of news is, "I am so sad to hear that your dog is sick." This type of comment will give you a safe place to express your grief rather than feeling like you have to take care of the other person's sadness.

The way you can react to this response is not to thank them. Because, remember, it is not your job to take care of someone else. Silence, a small smile, followed by a gentle head nod is all that is needed. If they persist, you can politely excuse yourself.

3. You are still grieving?

"You are still grieving?" is a very insensitive question to pose to someone that is feeling sad or depressed that his or her dog has a life-threatening illness. It suggests that there should be a time limit on the grief process and that you've taken it too far.

Prepare yourself by falling back on what you've learned about grief thus far in the book—grieving doesn't just go away, and it does not have a timetable. Remember, take as much time as is necessary with your grieving.

This question oftentimes helps people know who their real support team is. If you hear this, you can politely respond, "Yes I am," and then make your exit. You really don't want to waste your time with people that just don't get it.

4. Let me tell you what I did for my dog.

This is another tough one. Although it may seem supportive, it can also be overwhelming and create feelings of guilt. You just got the news about your dog, and you are still trying to figure out where all the pieces of the puzzle go in your new situation. Opening yourself up to a ton of advice at this time could be helpful, but it could also increase your feelings of anxiety, guilt, and hopelessness, and being overwhelmed.

By making your customized roadmap checklist (in chapter 2) and also designing daily and/or plans with goals on how you are going to take care of your dog, you can then pick and choose what advice you want to listen to. We will explore this in more detail in chapter 8.

A good way to respond to this fourth comment is, "I appreciate your thoughts of concern, but I really just need to process my feelings at this time."

Please use the three *Contemplative Questions* at the end of this chapter to guide you to become aware of and prepare your reaction to these kinds of statements.

Your Support Team

You are the expert when it comes to your grief journey and the caretaking of your dog. Your grief journey is unique, and no two people deal the same way with losing a dog to a life threatening-illness, such as cancer.

The important thing to remember is to choose the people that you interact with wisely during this special time. Choose those that truly support you, those that listen, don't judge you, and only give you advice when you ask them.

That type of support is available to you. You don't need to feel alone and go through this journey without support and compassion.

When you find these people, consider them friends to help you never have to walk the journey of pet loss grief alone again. In chapter 9, we will talk about ways in which you can get support.

Chapter Wrap-Up

This chapter is aimed to help you become aware of the unsupportive things that people are going to say to you while you are coping with your dog's illness. This is normal—and it is also normal for their words to trigger grief in you. The key to responding to such statements with compassion and grace is to prepare yourself and to entrench yourself in the truth about grief and its seven stages. You will use this chapter's *Contemplative Questions* to help you to become aware of and prepare your reaction to these statements.

Also, you may want to actively find one, two, or more people who will serve as your "support team," listening to you and allowing you to live out your grief as it naturally happens.

In the next chapter, I am going share with you why it is important to celebrate the life you have with your dog, even though you are experiencing intense grief. I will share tips and actual activities that you can do. When you celebrate the life you have with your dog, it is another way that you are supporting yourself on your grief journey in a healthy way.

Chapter Five Contemplation Questions

1. Which of the "Things That People Say" have you experienced? Feel free to write down others that are personal to you and have left you feeling more grief.

2. With each of the statements that you listed above, write down how you will respond to take control of the situation.

3. Can you list the ways in which you would like support with the pet grief that you are experiencing?

LIVING YOUR JOURNEY: SECTION TWO

Grief can be the garden of compassion. If you keep your heart open through everything, your pain can become your greatest ally in your life's search for love and wisdom.

—Rumi

6. Celebrating Life

Taking Stock

I would like to ask you right now a few questions to help prepare you for the next part of your pet grief journey—living your journey.

- Are you feeling that the life of your dog is so incredibly special?

- Do you want to provide the best care you can for him or her?

- Do you now understand that your pet grief is normal and okay?

- Are you allowing your feelings of grief to happen without feeling like you are crazy?

- Are you ready to take some action on helping your pet through this special time?

- Are you also ready to take care of yourself?

If you answered *yes* to any of these questions, then that is wonderful because one of the most important things about healing your pet grief is to take stock on where you are in the process.

All the chapters in this section are about taking action for what you are going to do next for your dog and yourself. They are not about stuffing your grief down. In fact, nowhere in this book am I going to encourage you to stuff your grief emotions.

Why? It is not a healthy way to do grief. As I've already explained, staying present with your grief is necessary and extremely healthy.

By knowing how you are going to spend your time with your dog during this journey, you are setting yourself up to cope proactively and positively with the myriad feelings that will come up during this time.

Grief emotions can be expected. Yet, the unexpected feelings of grief can rock your world if you are not prepared. And there are many more ways that I am going to continue to help you prepare in this book.

In previous chapters you learned to recognize your emotions of grief on physical, emotional, and spiritual levels. Plus you came to understand that your grief is unique to you, and it is normal.

Yet, there is so much more you can do for your healing to take place. So in your pet grief journey, you will take the time to celebrate the life of your dog while he or she is still alive. This can only enrich and deepen your bond.

This chapter is about how you can celebrate the life of your dog while your dog is still alive. It's about creating new adventures. Spending time with your dog in comfortable ways that focus around quality not quantity is key.

You may ask—why is this important? This process is another step to help heal your pet grief journey. If your dog only lives for one week or is fortunate enough to live for ten more months, you can still do all the activities in this chapter. This chapter will provide the guidance for you to begin to create more inner peace.

So many of my clients report that incorporating these suggestions into their daily plans has made them strong, more decisive, and more grounded on their grief journeys. They've been able to make tough decisions and deal with veterinarians more thoughtfully (something we'll address more in chapter 12).

Case Study — Sally and Larry

Sally, who was working with me in my Shoulder to Lean On support program, found that when she began to celebrate the life she had with her dog, Larry, she felt more at ease with what she was going through. It helped her feel more in control with her pet grief journey.

By actively and thoughtfully determining how she would celebrate Larry's life, Sally was actually able to do special things for Larry that made her feel really good.

One: How it worked is that Sally first made a list of all the things she and Larry had done together. For instance, Larry and Sally loved the beach, hiking mountains, training together, drives in the car, and snuggling on the couch. You name it! They were very active. She was amazed at all the activities and adventures they'd had together.

She felt incredibly healed by simply making a list of all their adventures and activities together.

Yet, after his diagnosis, Sally realized that Larry wasn't going to be able to hike mountains anymore. She took into consideration the current state of Larry's health to figure out what Larry could do. For example, they were still able to go to obedience classes, which was great. But she only did it if it didn't wear him out.

Two: At this point, Sally then made a new list that included new activities that matched Larry's abilities. Sally found that by doing this, she came up with some new ones that would be better suited for them. (In the next chapter, we will talk more about this in detail.)

Three: Sally spent time researching. She made lists of options for additional care to help Larry feel more comfortable. This helped Sally tremendously (we will cover this more in chapter 8).

The Importance of Celebrating

Let's face it—like Sally, you got terrible news about your dog, and your life is completely changing. You are probably feeling a lot of stress right now. As you know from the opening section of the book, what you are experiencing is normal. Your grief is active as a result of the changes that have occurred and the tough decisions that you must make.

A healthy and edifying way to express your grief, as Sally already demonstrated, is to celebrate the life that you and your dog had together. Make a list, write a story, and/or make a photo album that tells your adventures and activities together. This exercise will allow you to fully embrace the relationship that you have with your dog in a very healing way.

Use the three *Contemplation Questions* at the end of this chapter to help you prepare for the "Celebrate the Life" part of your unique pet grief journey.

You can thank your dog or express that you are sorry for any moment in your past that you wish had been different, for example, for not taking your dog out for a walk those days you were too busy. Again, as with the previous exercise, in doing this, you will allow yourself to fully embrace the relationship that you have with your dog in a very healing way by being present. Being present in your journey will help you create and spend time with those special moments that you have with your dog.

Provide your dog with comforting ways of assistance through this tough time in his or her life so that your dog can experience more comfort. Take care of yourself too so that you stay strong, healthy, and present to be there for your dog one hundred percent.

The chapters in this second section, *Living Your Journey*, will offer you more examples and options about how you can celebrate your dog and your life together. I'll be sharing tools that have helped so many of my clients, no matter how long their dogs lived.

Please try to incorporate as many of these suggestions as you can because you will be really happy that you did in the long run. I can promise you that your relationship with your special companion will deepen even more. The memories that you create will live within your heart forever. Those memories will never go away.

By actually doing these activities, you will ease the potential stress and strain of the grief journey because you took time to feel your grief. You created an action plan on how to live together during this special time before your dog dies.

Remember, this is an exceptional time for you and your dog. Cherish that and don't let anyone tell you that you are weird because you are caring for your pal in a very deep and caring way.

You are not weird. You are honoring and celebrating the life of your dog and your very special relationship. Your dog gave you a ton of love no matter what was going on in your life.

Stay focused and give the love back to your dog the way you want. If there are people in your life that are judging you, that is okay. Don't pay attention to them. Politely excuse yourself and go on with your business that focuses around your dog. You will be so happy that you did so. Your life with your dog will be enriched beyond belief.

Trust in the process and create the celebration of the life that you have with your dog by implementing the tools as Sally did for Larry. Invest in and cherish the journey for healing your pet grief.

Chapter Wrap-Up

In this chapter, I helped you become aware of why it is important to celebrate the life that you have right now with your dog, even though you are experiencing intense grief. You have the chapter's *Contemplation Questions* to help you prepare for the "Celebrate the Life" too.

You also learned that when you celebrate the life you have with your dog, you are also offering yourself support on your grief journey in a healthy way.

In the following chapter, I will share with you in more detail why it is important to celebrate the life you have with your dog by creating new adventures that are safe for your dog. I will share tips on how these adventures will create new memories that will help heal your pet grief.

Chapter Six Contemplation Questions

1. Now that you read this chapter and understand the importance of celebrating the life you have with your dog, identify the ways that you celebrate life with your dog. List the activities and adventures that you and your dog have done together.

2. What are the favorite activities that you can safely do now together?

3. What are some new or adapted activities that you can create now for you and your dog that will create new memories?

7. Planning New Adventures

You are grieving so many losses in regards to your relationship with your dog. Not only is your dog ill, but also the things that you two can do together are changing. Even though your dog is still with you right now, your daily routines have and will continue to change.

My goal is to help you find deeper enrichment with your dog during this special time. We are going to talk about creating some new adventures that you and your dog can share together. These activities don't have to be grandiose like climbing a mountain. They can be as simple as lying on the couch with your dog and taking a nap together.

We will concentrate on special activities that you two can do together and that, of course, will depend on your dog's health level at this time. (Please note that in the next chapter, I will talk more about some special ways that you can care for your dog's health.) Through these activities you will create new memories for the times that you two share during this special time. And through creating new adventures, you also give yourself the opportunity to reflect and love your dog in different ways, which, in turn, helps your grieving process.

The Importance of Quality

Before we get into the how, what, and when of your new activity plan, I would like to talk about quality. When healing your pet grief, a way to be truly effective and transformational is to spend the rest of your activity time totally focused on your dog.

What this means is, for example, if you are going out for ice cream cones, don't talk on your cell phone. Instead, spend quality time with your dog to enjoy every single lick of your ice cream together. If you are relaxing on the couch, instead of reading your email on your device, take a deep breath, touch your dog, and send loving energy to him or her.

Honestly, after your dog has died, you will think back to all the quality times that you gave your dog special attention. And any feelings of guilt may not even exist. Why? Because you participated fully with your dog while he or she was still in your life, and you were not distracted.

The Reminiscence List

The first thing that I ask my clients when we are working on this part of the healing pet grief journey is "What are the things that you like to do most with your dog?" Basically, I have them write out lists.

Your list can be any number of things that you love to do with your dog and what your dog likes to do. Include everything, don't edit or wonder if your dog can still do them at this point. I included a list template in Your Dog Grief Support Kit that you downloaded at the beginning of this book. I also gave you some examples in this chapter of some things you can include in this list.

The healing part of this exercise is that it gives you a chance to document and reminisce your relationship. You will probably discover things that you forgot that you did together but really enjoyed doing. You will remember some of your dog's toys, places, people, and other dogs that were part of both of your lives.

I will warn you that reminiscing about your adventures will bring up grief. Remember from previous chapters, especially the first and third, that it is okay and extremely healthy to feel pet grief.

Just keep in mind that what you are going through is normal and unique to your relationship with your dog. Going over these adventures will help you in many aspects of your grieving journey.

Here is an example of some of the things that Marcia included on her Reminiscence List. Marcia's list was a lot longer than this, but I'm only including an excerpt. You will learn more about Marcia and her dog, Murphy, later in this chapter.

Reminiscence List

Hiking the mountain 20 minutes from our home

Going to obedience classes

Hanging out with our friends

Picking out new collars

Sleeping in bed together

Doing errands together on Saturday morning

Playing in the first snow of the season

Sleeping on the couch together every Sunday afternoon

All our quiet times together

That time we spent a week at dog adventure camp

The New List

Now, make a new list that includes the things that you and your dog can actually now do together, even if your dog only has a very short time left. Include one or two things that you both enjoy and can do together. It might be as small as a scratch behind the ears. Know that that is okay. What you do with your dog is not about quantity at this stage; it is about the quality of the activity.

When making this second list, don't delete any of the activities that you wrote down in your first list. Keep the first list in a special place to save for later memories. (We will cover this more in my second book in *The Pet Bereavement Series*.)

Include any activities from your Reminiscence List that you and your dog can still do together on your new list of "Activities We Can Do" (also in Your Dog Grief Support Kit). Begin to go through this new list, making notes on which ones are your favorites.

Here is an example of Marcia's new list of "Activities We Can Do"—

Quiet times together

Snuggling on the coach on Sunday afternoon

Sleep in bed together

The Plan

Finally, make a plan. My clients find that the key for success when creating new adventures and for healing their pet grief is to create daily and weekly schedules to do the particular activities.

Depending on your schedule, you may only be able to allocate five minutes per day or up to five hours on certain days. For example, you could do something special like a five-minute body scratch where you are totally focused on your dog. Or maybe you have time and your dog has the ability for a five-hour exploration of some place new. The point is to plan ahead and actively decide how much time and exactly when each day that you will devote to being fully present with your dog.

If you love to walk on the beach, schedule it in your calendar. If your dog loves obedience classes and still is able to participate, keep that activity and schedule it in. If your dog is infirm yet one of your favorite activities together is to lie on the floor and cuddle, schedule that in as well.

You might be feeling that it is weird or unnecessary to schedule favorite activities. Please trust this process and understand why scheduling is important. With all the chaos that might be happening in your world right now, activities have a way of being forgotten. They get buried under the normal emotions associated with the grieving process—pain, stress, sadness, and confusion.

My clients who have taken the time to make their activity plans found that they not only had more enriching and quality time with their dogs, but their guilt was virtually non-existent after their dogs died.

To understand how important these lists and the plan are in supporting you in your grief journey, please spend some time reflecting on the three *Contemplation Questions* at the end of this chapter.

Case Study — Marcia and Murphy

Marcia did an amazing daily activity plan for her dog after she got notice that Murphy didn't have much longer to live. She called me immediately, and I helped her come up with a beautiful quality activity plan.

Murphy was very ill, and even though he wasn't ready for euthanasia, she wanted to be sure that the quality of Murphy's life was perfect.

She made her lists and came up with a daily plan. She carved out time to be sure to mindfully connect with Murphy by cooking him steak. She gave him a piece everyday while they sat on the floor together. This simple yet powerful activity was crucial for Marcia, and Murphy found incredible joy with his steak.

Even though sweet Mr. Murphy has died, Marcia still works with me in my Rescue Joy from Pet Loss Grief support program. During a phone call, she told me that this exercise helped her tremendously after Murphy reached the end of his life.

She found that by reading her original list, the Reminiscence List, over and over again, it gave her a tremendous feeling of relief and joy. She also felt that her guilt was the least of her grief feelings because she knew that she did the best she could for Murphy.

It may seem tedious or unnecessary to do these lists, but as you can see, it helped Marcia understand, process, and heal her grief. She eventually began to feel joy with the life that she shared with Murphy, and these lists helped her to do that.

Give yourself the time to do this activity just as Marcia did. I promise you it will be an invaluable tool for your journey of healing pet loss grief.

Chapter Wrap-Up

In this chapter, I helped you become aware of all the adventures that you and your dog shared together by creating an activity list, the Reminiscence List. You then created a new list of new adventures and memories that you can share together during this special time. You made a schedule to ensure that you allocate the time each day to doing these activities with your dog. Also, you know that the new activities can be very simple because the main point is quality, not quantity, and meeting your dog where he or she is actually at in terms of health.

Remember to visit the chapter's *Contemplation Questions* to understand how important these lists and the plan are in supporting you in your grief journey.

In chapter 8, I am going to share with you ways to help your pet feel more comfortable and hopefully suffer less anxiety during this time. You will also find out why it is important to include holistic health care in addition to regular medical care too.

Chapter Seven Contemplation Questions

1. After creating your first list, the Reminiscence List, that includes all the activities that you and your dog have enjoyed together, what feelings of grief are you experiencing?

2. After creating your second list, the "Activities We Can Do" list, which includes the activities that you can actually do now, what feelings of grief are you now experiencing?

3. When you create your daily/weekly/monthly activity plan, how do your grief feelings change? How do your pet grief feelings change after you have done some of these activities?

8. Health Care and Your Dog

Many of my clients search for multiple ways to take action to find the best health care possible for their terminally ill dogs. It's important to them to get things into gear as soon as they can, so their dogs can feel as comfortable as possible, given their dogs' conditions. These clients want to be sure that they do the best they can for their dogs and provide all the health care possible.

Integrative health care for terminally ill animals is an area of great personal interest (and experience) to me. Aiding clients in finding the most supportive healthcare teams for their terminally ill dogs is something I really enjoy and have vast experience doing. In fact, it is how my work as a massage therapist for humans, horses, and hounds developed into working with people and their terminally ill pets.

It is important when your dog is diagnosed with a life-threatening illness to get a good team of professionals on your side for your dog. When considering integrative veterinarian medicine, think about including a regular veterinarian, a holistic veterinarian, as well as other healthcare professionals.

One of the most important things to remember is to pick your team wisely. Be sure that everyone is on your side and has your dog in their best interests. If someone on your professional team is not willing to respect your decisions and wishes, then it is time to find someone who will.

Case Study — Isabelle and Misty

When Isabelle was ready to put Misty's healthcare team together, I coached her with this first task—finding a regular medical veterinarian that she trusted, that communicated well, and that respected her journey and choices.

Since Isabelle's current veterinarian didn't respect some of her holistic choices, she had to find a new veterinarian, but that was okay. It was the best for her and Misty during their journey.

Having a regular veterinarian and specialists on board can be useful when it comes to diagnosis, emergencies, and other tasks your holistic veterinarian may not include in his or her scope of practice.

Since Isabelle wanted to integrate holistic medicine, I then guided her to do some research to locate a good holistic veterinarian. This took a little time, but within a week she found one that had experience. Plus, the person absolutely loved Misty.

The added bonus was that her medical veterinarian was willing to communicate to her holistic veterinarian. This helped Isabelle because she didn't need to waste valuable time with an unsupportive team member. Both of these veterinarians were willing to work together, which gave Isabelle peace of mind.

A Healthcare Team— Medical and More

Having a healthcare team is a crucial first step to consider when you get the news that your dog is terminally ill. Yet, your healthcare team doesn't need to end with just the medical profession. There are many other types of holistic care professionals that you may want to consider adding to your team.

Massage Therapy

Having a trained canine massage therapist on your team can be helpful for a variety of reasons. Massage can help your dog relax and feel more comfortable if there is any pain. The pain may not be from the illness itself. The fact is your dog might not be able to use his or her muscles like before, and the inactivity causes the muscles to become sore and stiff.

A gentle massage keeps the circulation moving. Massage can help with the removal of toxins in the bloodstream and allows for healthier muscle tissue. My dog clients love their massages.

Animal Reiki or Energy Practitioner

The other team member you might want to include is an animal Reiki practitioner or a practitioner that practices other forms of energy healing.

Reiki can balance your dog's energy and help him or her feel relaxed and calm, and suffer from less anxiety during this time. When I work on my canine clients with Reiki or other forms of energy techniques, they begin to breathe more deeply, relax more, and settle into very calm states of mind.

There are many other forms of energy work that are extremely beneficial and that you may want to consider. Integrative Manual Therapy (IMT) and Tellington TTouch are two others that I incorporate into my practice with great results.

Acupressure or Acupuncture

Both of these modalities are extremely helpful. Acupuncture is where tiny needles are placed in strategic points to balance your pet's energy. Acupressure uses the same spots with a thumb rather than a needle.

Both of these techniques have excellent results for a variety of issues. Relieving pain, increasing mobility, and lowering stress are just a few of the benefits that acupressure or acupuncture can provide.

Herbal Medicine

Herbal medicine is a great way to support a dog with a terminal illness. Herbs can help with supporting the immune system, pain relief, digestion, and more. My dog, Marley, was on a Chinese herb that actually shrunk tumors associated with nasosarcoma.

How to Choose

The three *Contemplative Questions* at the end of this chapter will help you choose the most appropriate and capable members of the healthcare team for your dog.

Please take the time to visit those questions and respond to them fully.

Without Delay

There are so many more options for you to consider when building your team. It can take some time and some patience, so I encourage all my clients, whether via in-person, phone, or SKYPE consultations, to begin this process right away.

The important thing to remember when assembling your healthcare team is to choose a team that has the proper training, experience, and credentials.

For example, a human massage therapist not trained in canine anatomy could cause harm due to the fact the person does not know how the canine body functions. The same applies for energy work, acupuncture, Reiki, etc. Special training to apply these therapies to animals is necessary.

Case Study — Jeannie and Oreo

I would like to tell you another story of a beautiful dog that came to me with a tumor in his right shoulder. Oreo was a beautiful Border Collie that loved his massages.

When Jeannie found out Oreo had cancer, she immediately called me. She wanted to help him feel better so that he would be able to lead his life with less pain.

Oreo came weekly for ten months. When he first came, his muscles were so rigid from the fact that he was limping, which then was throwing his active body off alignment.

Yet, when the time came that his leg needed to be amputated, his muscle health was in excellent shape. Even though his daily exercise had been compromised, his muscles were still healthy because of the benefits of massage therapy.

The transition for him was easier because his muscle health was excellent. Oreo was with me for ten months. He went through chemo like a champ and lived every day with sheer pleasure.

I was honored to be able to visit Oreo on the day that he was going to be euthanized. Even on that day, when I gave him his massage, he looked at me with his dark rheumy eyes, emitting both balance and grace.

The Merit of Teamwork

By taking some time to get your team together, it can help you walk your journey of pet grief with a feeling of strength and purpose.

My clients often comment that after their dogs have died, they feel so grateful they did this. They don't feel guilty about not doing enough for their dogs. They did everything just right.

In fact some felt that because they had strong teams that consisted of a regular veterinarian, holistic veterinarian, canine massage therapist, and a person trained in energy work, they are convinced their dogs got the best care possible.

That feeling of accomplishment allowed them to not feel guilty. Feeling guilty after you dog dies, or even while your dog is alive, is a normal feeling of grief. Yet, it happens more when you don't go into action while your dog is still alive.

By understanding your grief (first, third, and fourth chapters), choosing your friends that are going to support you (fifth chapter), spending quality time with your dog while he or she is still alive (seventh chapter), and picking a support team based on the needs of your pet (current chapter), you will feel like you did all that you could. You will be offering your beloved dog your utmost support, and you will be offering yourself the same.

The clients who choose to find the best teams possible are the ones that say, "I gave my dog the best care I could, and I feel really good about that."

Chapter Wrap-Up

Finding the proper health care for your dog is critical to the process of not only helping your dog feel better but to helping you with your grief process as well. Your healthcare team will be composed not only of the veterinarian, but also of holistic animal healthcare practitioners.

Choosing practitioners that respect you, your dog, and your choices is essential. Take the time to research, interview, and get referrals for the practitioners that you choose to be on your team. Use the chapter's *Contemplative Questions* to assist you too. This careful consideration and building of the healthcare team will help both your dog in his or her last days, months, and years, and you on your grief journey.

In the next chapter, I am going to share with you tips on how to take care of yourself—in areas that do not include your dog. I am going to give you reasons and examples of ways in which you can restore yourself during this special time. Plus, you will also learn that it is okay to want take some alone time away from your dog.

Chapter Eight Contemplation Questions

1. What are some holistic modalities that you would like to include for helping your dog? Massage? Energy work? Acupuncture? Something else?

2. Do you feel comfortable asking your regular medical veterinarian if he or she would be on your team if you wanted to include a holistic veterinarian? What makes you comfortable or uncomfortable about asking? What can you do to feel more comfortable asking this question?

3. Make a list of the questions that you would ask each member of your team. They may include:

-   Do you support holistic veterinarian medicine?

- Are you willing to communicate with other members of the healthcare team?

- What is your training in?

- How much experience do you have?

- Are you credentialed and/or licensed?

- Do you have any clients whom I can talk to about the work you do?

9. Caring for Yourself

When you get the news that your dog is going to die, your first response may very well be that you want to spend 24/7 with your dog because you just don't know how much time you may have left with him or her. This is a normal response.

However, allowing time in your schedule for self-care that does not involve your dog will actually make the time you do spend with him or her have greater quality.

While all of my clients feel the guiltiest about taking time away from their dogs to care for themselves, everyone needs to know that it is totally okay to do this. Not only is it okay, it is necessary. Self-care is actually a great way to manage your pet grief journey to allow greater focus, strength, and compassion to shine through.

Case Study — Annie and Spot

In the beginning Annie felt she must devote all her free time to her dog, Spot. She didn't sleep, and she stopped exercising. In a short period of time, she was completely exhausted and suffered with one cold after another.

What had happened? Annie stopped allowing time for herself.

When Annie shared all this with me, we set up a self-care plan that was doable for her. With this plan she was able to experience some wonderful changes. She stopped getting colds, her grief was less intense, and she was able to be more present to Spot in his last weeks. Plus, when faced with a really tough decision, she felt in control to do the best she could.

The Best Advice

Now please listen closely to the best advice that I can give you right now and that I gave to Annie—carve out time to replenish your own body, mind, and soul. It's necessary and important.

You can give your dog a ton of attention during this special time. Yet, if you are tired, burned-out, stressed-out, not eating, and not sleeping because you feel the need to be with your dog 24/7, then the quality of that time will suffer and important decisions will be difficult to make.

This is the time to take care of yourself so that you are functioning at the best you can and not relying on your reserve.

Like Annie discovered, having strength is critical for you to be ready for the unexpected feelings of grief, the emergencies, and the challenging medical decisions you must make.

The "What" of Self-Care

There are many things that you can do for yourself that don't cost a lot of money, like walking in nature, taking a nap, taking a bath, hanging out with friends, listening to relaxing music, or having a cup of tea.

The important thing is to create a self-care plan that you know you can do. It's not important how many things you have on your list. The important thing is to create success for yourself. Include new activities that you would love to experience and old activities that have already given you joy and grounding.

In previous chapters and even in the next chapters, we will continue to explore more ways of honoring your dog, but for now just focus on yourself.

Remember the healthier you are in body, mind, and spirit, the easier it is to cope and deal with the grief that you are going through and to be present for you dog in his or her final period of life.

The Physical Self

Let's talk about some of the options for taking care of your physical body during this time. These activities that you do for yourself are not in combination with the activities that you are doing with your dog right now.

This is about time for you!

My clients find that when they do one or more of the following physical things for their bodies, they feel stronger and more in control of their grief. Even if they can do something for only five to ten minutes a day, it still helped them in their journeys.

I will suggest to you to spend at least a half hour every day if you can with any combination of the following activities for the health of your body.

- Massage

- Walks in nature

- Reiki or other form of energy bodywork

- Exercise class

- Eat well and throughout the day

- Get your sleep

- Take short breaks throughout the day with your eyes closed

- Breathe intentionally and actively

If a half hour every day is too much time, try to give yourself a half hour at least three times a week taking care of your physical body.

The Mental Self

The next thing to take care of is your mind. As you know, your mind is going in a million different directions right now. Sometimes your mind clutter is creating so much anxiety and stress, you wonder how you are going to get through this.

To help your mind, you can find support groups, pet loss grief coaches, psychotherapists, friends, coworkers, family members, and veterinarians that totally respect the journey of pet grief that you are going through. They should be there for you and be able to walk this journey with you so that you don't have to feel alone.

Finding ways to support your mind's health can take some time, but if you know what you are looking for, the process can be less stressful.

Here are some of the ways that you can create a healthy mind that can support you.

- Talk to a pet grief coach—a coach will listen and allow you to better manage your healing process.

- Talk to a psychotherapist or other healthcare provider—it is important to find someone that gets pet loss.

- Pet loss support groups—these provide another way to support you. In them you will meet people that are going through similar situations. Be sure you find one where you feel that you are getting ample time to express your journey and are not being judged by anyone.

- Friends and family—this is a tough one. Your friends and family may mean well, yet they may also be the ones that trigger your grief because they really don't know how to support you. Choose wisely and choose only those friends and family that let you talk and that don't offer advice. Definitely stay away from the ones that judge you!

A healthy mind is a strong mind that creates balance when your mind clutter starts getting out of hand. Having a support system helps you monitor your mind and offers solutions when your grief is swirling out of control.

Choose a couple of these options that feel good to you. Do some research and don't feel bad if the person that you thought was your best friend doesn't support you. There is someone that will!

The Spiritual Self

Now let's talk about your spiritual health. Many times you can forget about this one when experiencing pet grief. You may even be uncomfortable with your spiritual beliefs or may not have any.

Whatever your spiritual choice, remember it is your journey. I encourage you to only incorporate a spiritual practice into your daily life if you feel comfortable.

Here are some of the ways that you can create spiritual health in your life.

- Meditation comes in all forms. A quiet walk in the woods is equally meditative as sitting quietly in one posture clearing your mind of all thoughts.

- Yoga, tai chi, or other forms of spiritual physical practice help your body become stronger. The discipline and focus create a connection to your inner spiritual force.

- Your spiritual belief, no matter what your belief is, the daily, weekly, or periodic practice of it can help you receive solace.

- An animal communicator is a great way to get peace of mind and learn the spiritual connection that you have with your dog from your dog's perspective.

I have shared with you many ways to take care of yourself. It is totally up to you on how you would like to include one or many of the suggestions that I offered.

Remember this is a trying time for you. You are getting bombarded with so much information, and the stress may be wearing you down.

Creating a support team for yourself is equally important as creating a support team for your dog (from chapter 8). Taking care of yourself is important because you want to provide the best you can for your dog. It is difficult to do that if you are tired, hungry, stressed-out, suffering from body aches, and more.

Use the three *Contemplation Questions* at the end of the chapter to take action for your own self-care without guilt. Even if the only thing you can do right now is simple breathing to create balance in your life, that is okay!

Chapter Wrap-Up

In this chapter I shared ways that helped so many of my clients find peace of mind and strength. I encouraged you to take some time for yourself without feeling guilty. Care for yourself in terms of your body, mind, and spirit.

By allowing time in your schedule for self-care, you will be able to spend more quality time with your dog. You'll make better decisions and be ready for unexpected grief too, just as was true for my client Annie.

Remember to use the three *Contemplation Questions* to determine the what, when, and how of your own self-care.

In the next chapter, I am going to offer support for when you have the feeling that you just can't do enough for your dog. You will learn how to deal with the overwhelming feelings of guilt and anger, as well as other forms of pet grief, when you feel like you just haven't done enough. Plus, it is a sure-fire way to let your dog know that you love him or her.

Chapter Nine Contemplation Questions

1. What is one or two activities that you can do to take care of your physical body this week?

2. What is one or two ways that you can reach out to get support for the health of your feelings and thoughts (mind)?

3. If you are a spiritual person and have gotten away from your practice, how can you begin incorporating your beliefs into your everyday life?

10. Saying Thank You

If you are feeling like you are not sure of what else you can do for your dog or if you are feeling stuck and even suffering with guilt that you are not doing enough for your dog, I would like to assure you that your feelings are normal. You are not alone, and these feelings are part of the pet grief journey. In fact, you are exactly in the right place with your pet grief.

When my clients reach this point of feeling overwhelmed, I suggest that they begin telling their dogs, "Thank you for everything that you gave me in life."

As a passionate dog lover, you probably do this already. Yet there are ways to talk with your dog that can create a sense of being listened to and understood. That's what I want to teach you to do.

It really isn't that hard, and I teach people all over the world to do it.

What to Do + A Case Study — Shirley and Peanuts

This is a special time for you and your dog. Creating a comfortable, peaceful, and healing journey for the both of you is one of the most important things to consider.

It is important to ask yourself, "How am I going to strengthen my relationship so that when the end of my dog's life is imminent, I am able to participate fully? How am I going to give everything I can to my dog as he or she reaches the end of life?"

First Step: Let's begin by setting some intentions or goals on what you would like to tell your dog. I am going to share with you how Shirley planned to begin talking with her dog, Peanuts.

Shirley and I had a few conversations in my Shoulder to Lean On program because she wanted to be sure that she was thorough. She didn't want to leave anything out of the conversation.

I am going to share with you five of the most critical things on Shirley's list.

1. How am I going to say thank you to Peanuts while she is still alive?

2. What are the ways that I am going to tell her that I am sorry?

3. How am I going to tell Peanuts that I love her?

4. What are the important lessons that Peanuts taught me?

5. How am I going to tell Peanuts that I will be okay when she dies and to not worry about me?

Please feel free to use these for your own planning. Also, use the *Contemplation Questions* at the end of the chapter when creating the things that you want to tell your dog.

After Shirley had her list on paper, she read it out loud a few times to herself. She experienced grief yet channeled her feelings of grief to answer her questions.

You can do this as well. After you choose any of questions above or even some of your own, write them down. Say them out loud a few times. Allow your feelings of grief to happen. And at the same time, use these strong feelings to guide you in finding the most complete answers to the questions.

Remember your feelings and emotions are normal, and it is very important to let them out rather than stuff them in.

One of the biggest regrets that I hear from people who come to me after their dogs have died is that they wish they'd told their pets how much they loved them. They wish they'd thanked them for sharing life with them. Many even are painfully sorry that they missed a few walks.

If you do this activity now, you will feel better about your journey in the future. Shirley was so happy that she spent the time doing this for Peanuts.

Step Two: Decide when and where you will have the conversation.

You now have a list of what you would like to share and tell your dog. Are you wondering how to do it? Are you wondering if your dog is going to understand you?

Rest assured that your dog does understand you. Your dog is an expert with reading your body language, hearing your voice, and understanding you better than anyone. No need to worry that he or she won't understand or hear you.

Instead, your job is to create a special time so that you can respectfully talk to your dog. This is not to say that you can't talk to your dog while walking, snuggling on the couch, or playing on the beach. Any type of communication is fine whenever the mood strikes you.

Yet for deeper healing purposes, it is important to take time out from your busy day to create calm. Be totally focused for sharing the things that you want to share with your dog.

I would recommend going to a place with your dog where you will not be disturbed. This place may be a beautiful setting in nature or a quiet room in your home. Try and keep the activity relaxed rather than playing with a ball or stick.

Shirley took Peanuts to the beach. They sat in the car while she told Peanuts how much she loved her.

The beauty of this is that you are setting the stage for some deep, meaningful communication. You are also actively healing your pet grief. Plus you are sharing an adventure together as we discussed earlier in chapter 7.

Step Three: Once you have chosen the place where you would like to talk with your dog and you know that you will not be disturbed, look into the eyes of your dog and smile. It is okay to touch and cuddle your dog too.

Then close your eyes and take a few deep breaths. Settle the chaos in your mind and relax. I have a great meditation for you to download on my website (you can find the link for this gift in the Resources section of this book) for free that can help you with this. Once you are calm and ready, begin to talk to your dog.

If you choose to tell your dog that you love him or her, also explain all the things about him or her that you love. Talk to your dog as you would another adult. Try to not baby talk as it dilutes the power of your intention.

The important thing is that you are talking to your dog and making a conscious effort to tell him or her everything that he or she means to you.

Something else to consider is that you can do this more than one time. You can have this same talk with your dog as many times as you like. For example, Shirley had conversations like this with Peanuts every morning after breakfast.

Extreme Healing

This exercise is extremely healing. Yet as you talk to your dog, your grief feelings will probably begin to come alive again.

Remember grief is normal, and it is part of life. Allow your feelings of grief to come out. Tell your dog what you are feeling. Your dog is your best friend and even though he or she is ill, your dog still wants connection with you.

So much healing can take place with this activity. And my clients are so thankful when they reflect back to this time. They often comment how glad they are that they changed the way they talked to their dogs.

Shirley was so happy that she got a chance to tell Peanuts that she was sorry and that she loved her.

The Difficult One

One of the biggest successes is from those clients that told their dogs, "I will be okay, and it is okay to die."

This is a difficult one. Because really, are you going to be okay after your dog dies?

I wasn't! I threw my bicycle in the woods and was super angry with my deities for taking away such an amazing, healthy dog to cancer! How could they?

But the important thing is Marley knew that in the long run, I was going to be okay. I honestly told her that during her illness.

I told her that it was okay for her to die when she was ready. I told her I was thankful for all she did for me. Marley taught me to choose happiness in my life with joy in her teachings.

Chapter Wrap-Up

It is normal to experience overwhelming feelings that you are not doing enough for your dog. Know that these are normal, and also take action. By talking to your dog in a well-planned way, you will be able to cope with those extreme pet grief feelings.

Remember how healing and powerful this talking experience was for Shirley and Peanuts, as well as for Marley and me.

Use the three *Contemplation Questions* to help you design, plan, and implement your special conversation with your dog.

In the next chapter we will address the tough decisions you'll likely encounter as your dog reaches the end of life. You will begin to learn how to be prepared for this very difficult time.

Chapter Ten Contemplation Questions

1. Now that you read about Shirley and Peanuts, what do you want to tell your dog? List everything that you want to say to your dog.

2. As you make your list, what are the feelings of grief coming up for you?

3. Where is your special place that you are going to tell your dog the things that you want to say? How are you going to tell your dog?

ENDING YOUR JOURNEY: SECTION THREE

Grief changes shape, but it never ends.

—Keanu Reeves

11. Last Day Preparation

Probably the last thing that you want to think about right now is how you are going to prepare for the last day of your dog's life.

Are you asking yourself, "Isn't it enough to feel and get in touch with my grief? Won't being in touch with my grief help me during these last few days, hours, moments, and even after my dog dies?"

Yes, it will! It is very important to know and understand everything that you are going through to heal your pet loss. Yet, I can promise you that if you spend some additional time preparing for your dog's last day, you will have a different experience.

This experience will leave you knowing that you did the best you could for your dog. Therefore, you may experience less chaos because you know that you were prepared for this day.

In this section I am going to support you with making some tough decisions about dealing with this part of your grief journey. I am going to share some amazing tools that my clients have used over and over again to help guide them through this extremely tough time.

Quick Recap

You have come a long way and have created some amazing adventures with your dog. These incredible memories will bring many moments of joy to your soul.

Understanding that grief is not only normal but also that how you experience it is unique is imperative. It is vital to the relationship that you have with your dog right now.

You also know that it is healthy to experience grief and that it is something you cannot avoid. To express your pet grief in the various ways talked about in this book, you will walk the grief journey with incredible personal empowerment. Plus, you may even find some joy in your process, which we will talk about in chapter 15.

Let's begin to explore how you can do this by preparing for the last day of your dog's life.

The Stages of Final Day Preparation

As with the rest of the grief process, preparation for the last day of your dog's life comes in stages. I am going to help you be prepared for these stages in the next few chapters.

Chapter Twelve—Preparing your plan ahead of time will help you make some really tough decisions. One of the biggest and most avoided considerations that my clients face as they spend the last few days, weeks, or months with their dog is "When is the right time to euthanize my dog?"

If you are stressing over this decision, know that you are not alone. All of my clients stress over this question each time their dogs are approaching the end of their lives.

The final act from this decision is permanent, and for all good reasons you want to make sure your timing is perfect. We will talk about this more in chapter 12. I will support you with ways to help you prepare and make this difficult decision with less stress and anxiety.

Chapter Thirteen—We are going to spend time writing a love letter to your dog. This letter will be a proclamation of appreciation, healing, and apology (if needed). It will also include anything else that you might want to express to your dog at the time of death.

I will share with you the importance of writing something down and then reading it to your dog at the time of death to increase your heart connection. It will also help you with any lingering pet loss grief feelings of guilt, denial, and anxiety.

Chapter Fourteen—It is also important for you to know what you can expect after your dog reaches the end of his or her life. I am going to help you be prepared for your grief through the death experience in chapter 14. It is somewhat similar to what you have been coping with currently with your dog. Yet there are some very important changes to be aware of for your healing. For example, people around you are going to react differently, and your expectations for your own behavior are going to increase.

I am going to guide you to be prepared for this time when your soul feels empty and loneliness settles in.

Chapter Fifteen—Finally, I offer supportive tools that will guide you on what you can do next. Expectations are still going to increase from the people around you and for yourself.

This period does take time to adjust to, and we will talk about ways that you can move through it with grace and compassion for yourself.

To begin preparing for your dog's final day, please take time to respond to the three *Contemplation Questions* at the end of the chapter.

Case Study — Mary and Luna

The pet loss grief journey is one of the most profound experiences that you can have. There is no human that can give you so much love as your dog did.

I am sure you have people in your life that love you tremendously and you love them. But do you really have anyone in your life that loves you unconditionally, without judgment?

Mary realized that she had a lot of people in her life that supported her with the grief of losing her dog, Luna. She knew her friends and family members loved her. Yet, she told me that even though they all loved her and gave her a ton of support, they still judged her when she was going through a really tough time.

Mary told me, "Luna was an incredible force in my life. She loved me when I was going through a tough time without judgment. She would snuggle with me and look at me with adoring eyes. She taught me about love. She didn't care if I stayed in my pajamas all day like my family did. Luna loved me for who I was and what I had become. She taught me to become a better person."

Mary learned that the lessons Luna showed her were some of the greatest gifts that she could ever receive. Mary experienced life-changing moments with Luna's unconditional love. She learned that she did not need to judge herself even though others did.

The unconditional love that Luna expressed to Mary provided Mary with the confidence to know that she was doing the best she could.

The Goal of Preparation

Another point that I would love for you to consider is that your feelings of personal grief will be incredibly strong when the last day of your dog's life comes.

My goal is to help you be prepared when this last day arrives, so those decisions do not have to be made at the last minute. You already know what you are going to do. You have a plan that you feel good about. There will be less chaos in your life.

My goal is that when this day comes, you can look into your dog's eyes and know that it is time. Your plan is your self-support tool that will help you stay clear and present. You will be able to be completely attentive to the needs of your dog, rather than making last-minute decisions. You don't want lose out on a very special moment in your journey with your dog.

When your dog reaches the end of his or her life, this is the time that you do not want to be scrambling. It is a time for you to be there for your dog as he or she may be going through fear and anxiety.

This is a special time because the more you can be attentive to your dog's needs, the better you will feel after your dog is no longer in your life.

Chapter Wrap-Up

You've begun to realize how important it is to have a plan of action so that you can be prepared for the myriad decisions that you will have to make in the final day of your dog's life.

You also learned that your dog gives you unconditional love without judgment and how that can make you a better person. Mary and Luna's story exemplified this powerful relationship.

Use the three *Contemplation Questions* to begin to prepare for your dog's last day.

In the next chapter you will learn how to make some tough decisions for your dog. This will help you feel more control during a very chaotic time. The next chapter will guide you through the process of preparation for the last day so that you feel prepared for this extremely tough time.

Chapter Eleven Contemplation Questions

1. Now that you read about Mary and Luna, how does your dog support you with unconditional love?

2. As you list these ways of support from your dog, what feelings of grief come up for you? How do you feel about these feelings?

3. What are some of the ways in which you have become a better person because of your dog?

12. Tough Decisions

One of the biggest decisions and the most anxiety-producing question that I get from my clients is "When do I know the time is right to euthanize my dog?"

This decision is by far a very difficult one, and as decisions go, no one really wants to make this one at the wrong time. Yet, this decision is a crucial one.

When you determine early in your pet loss journey how you are going to deal with euthanasia, it can help you stay focused on your pet when he or she needs you the most. This time can be extremely chaotic, and the last thing you want to be doing is making a spur-of-the-moment decision.

The Two Big Questions

When Judy was ready to talk to me about making this decision for her dog, Ruby, she had two main questions. These same two questions are the ones that most of my clients have asked me.

You may be asking yourself these questions as well . . . .

1. How do I know when the right time is?

2. When is the best time to euthanize my dog?

Although these questions are tough, they are excellent. And by answering them in your unique way, it will help you with many of the grief stages and emotions that you are going through.

Question One

Let's start with the first one, "How do I know when the right time is?" It's a hard question. At first, no one can really answer it without doubt and without questioning if his or her answer is correct.

Yet, with Judy's experience with Ruby, my own experiences with my own pet loss, and the experiences of many of my clients, I can tell you that when you are clear with your answer, it can help you feel incredibly connected to your dog.

Knowing the answer to this question and not doubting your decision will also help with some of the most prevalent feelings of grief, such as guilt, anxiety, anger, and depression.

When is the right time?

First—ask for your veterinarian's opinion. If you have more than one veterinarian, ask each and every one of them. They deal with pet loss almost every day. Their experienced answers can guide you with the first stage of answering this question for you and your dog.

They will probably give you the following answers. I encourage you to explore your feelings with each of these options.

The time is right . . .

- when the quality of life of your dog is no longer the way it was

- when your dog is in a lot of pain

- when your dog can't walk

- when your dog is unable to respond

- when your dog's bodily functions are no longer functioning or not under your dog's control

- when your dog loses his or her dignity

- when your dog tells you

All of these answers are useful and extremely important for you to consider. Yet they do not take into consideration your process and the unique relationship that you have with your dog. This is important for you to consider before your dog is approaching the end of life.

Second—if you have a great support team, ask them. They can offer you a lot of support.

It isn't worth it if you ask people that don't understand what you are going through. This lack of support will only create more stress and anxiety around your decision-making.

Third—if you are working with a pet loss grief coach, be sure to spend time exploring this topic. Your coach will help you set up a unique plan that will support you with making the best decision around this topic, as well as other topics, in a meaningful way.

Something to keep in mind is that you may be asking the opinion of others. Even though these are important opinions, remember you are the one who lives with and cares for your dog every single day. Along with these opinions, you and your dog will know best.

Many of my clients are thankful for this exercise early in their pet loss journeys, even though it is a difficult decision to make.

Please note—if your grief feelings are affecting you so much that you have suicidal thoughts or you are unable to function, seeing a psychotherapist or medical practitioner is a necessary choice for you at this time.

Question Two

When is the right time to euthanize my dog?

You have collected the opinions of your veterinarians and you know your dog better than anyone. You know when your dog is uncomfortable or is resting quietly. You know when your dog is happy or sad. You know when your dog is in pain and struggling through life.

You can just look into his or her eyes and know what your dog is saying to you. Right?

Once you have your veterinarian's opinion and worked on your own feelings about the end-of-life process, it is now time to ask your dog.

Asking Maya

When my first dog, Maya, was dying from cancer, I asked my holistic veterinarian on the way to the emergency hospital, "How will I know?" She told me the best way to know is to ask Maya, "She will tell you."

That was the best advice I could have ever gotten from anyone. It was pivotal in calming the chaos as my husband

and I drove two hours to the specialty hospital where Maya was being treated.

When we got to the hospital, we rushed in to see her, and I looked into her eyes and they looked different. The brightness was no longer there, and all I could see was pain, so I asked, "Maya, are you ready?" I got the overwhelming feeling that she was, just by the way she looked at me.

I am not saying here that this was easy. Yet, I didn't question myself. Instead, I trusted the relationship that I had with Maya and what she had to tell me.

You know the relationship that I am talking about. It is the same one that you have with your dog that is based on trust and mutual respect.

The Human-Animal Bond

We are their caretakers from the moment they set their paws into our homes. They are our family. The human-animal bond is different than what we have with our friends and other family members.

Your dog trusts you to make the best decisions for him or her that are based on the life that you spent together. When the time comes, be prepared for your dog.

Don't wait until your dog has reached the end of his or her life to make these decisions. Take the time now to determine the answers to these questions, even though it is extremely hard and may bring up more feelings of grief that you would like to avoid.

Work with the three *Contemplation Questions* at the end of this chapter to receive further guidance in this process so that you know that you made the right decision at the right time.

Judy has been extremely thankful and happy she answered these questions early on. By doing so, she felt extremely prepared and present for Ruby when the time came. She had a lot less guilt and panic. She didn't have to scramble during a potentially chaotic time.

Instead, she was able to give Ruby her full attention during her euthanasia.

Chapter Wrap-Up

In this chapter we talked about ways in which you can get support for making one of the toughest decisions you will ever have to make for your dog. Although it may be painful, it will be so much more beneficial to you and your dog for you to work out your answers to these two tough questions early on.

I shared with you seven tips that can help you make this decision in a very meaningful way. Use this advice to help and guide you during this very difficult time. Also use the three *Contemplation Questions* to help ensure that you make the right decision at the right time.

In chapter 13 I am going to show you how you can proclaim in a very special way your appreciation, love, and respect for your dog. This tool will give you a way to heal any regrets that you may have for not giving your pet more time or energy.

Chapter Twelve Contemplation Questions

1. What are your feelings about each of the seven tips that I shared about making a decision about euthanasia?

2. What feelings of pet grief come up for you when you reflect on these tips?

3. What tips are you going to pay most attention to during this special time that you have with your dog?

13. Love Letter

If you are at the point in your journey where you want to do something very special for your dog that will last forever, that is wonderful.

Maybe you would like to create a very different way to tell your dog how much you love him or her. However, your mind clutter may be a little chaotic with all your thoughts and feelings at this point. Remember that is okay.

It doesn't matter where you are in your journey because writing a love letter to your dog at any time is a wonderful way to heal your pet grief.

When you can collect and express the love that you have for your dog in a love letter, it is extremely helpful for your pet grief journey.

Are you not sure where to begin?

That is okay. I am going to help you and encourage you to spend some time everyday jotting down special memories or things that you want to tell your dog.

Even spending only five to ten minutes a day writing down some special memories will help you. It will lead to your writing a personal and meaningful love letter to your dog.

Keep in mind this is your proclamation of appreciation, healing, apology (if needed), and inclusion of anything else that you may want to express to your dog before the time of death.

Yet, if there is not time for you to do this before your dog reaches the end of his or her life, that is okay too. It is still an incredibly healing process to do even after your dog dies.

My clients who work with me in my Rescue Joy from Pet Loss Grief program have found healing and solace no matter when they wrote their love letters. In my course, clients write a series of letters that help them move through coping with pet loss with grace, respect, and compassion for themselves.

Case Study — Michelle and Igor

You may be asking, "Why should I write things down and read it to my dog?" That is a common question, and often writing is not a favorite activity—until you write your first letter.

Michelle found this when she wrote her letter to her dog, Igor. Michelle discovered how important it was to put her thoughts and feelings down on paper.

She hated to write, but when she started to jot down special memories that she shared with Igor, she changed her mind.

After she collected all her thoughts, she wrote her love letter to Igor. She read it to him out loud and later told me, "Writing and reading my love letter to Igor increased the love that I have for him. It helped me celebrate our life together. It made it really special."

Michelle experienced this exercise as a proclamation to her dog. Writing a love letter and then reading it out loud helped her with any lingering feelings of pet grief, such as guilt, denial, and anxiety that she had been experiencing.

Step 1 — Essential Questions

Here are some questions that I share with my clients who are working through the Rescue Joy from Pet Loss Grief program. Each week there are about ten to twelve questions that encourage and support them through this tough time.

These questions will also help you pinpoint the feelings of compassion and love that you have for your dog.

Before you answer these questions, have a designated place where you will write your answers. It may be a special journal, your computer, or just a piece of paper.

Be sure to keep all of your answers in one place so that when you are ready to write your love letter, you have everything in front of you.

1. What did it feel like when you first met your dog?

2. How did you choose to bring your dog home?

3. What were the things that you love to do for your pet as the caretaker?

4. What are you sorry for, and how can you apologize to your dog?

There is no need to answer these questions all at once unless you are really motivated to do so. When you answer these questions, keep in mind that no one is going to read them except you. Write down whatever comes to your mind without judgment and editing.

The important thing is to get your feelings out on paper so that you are ready to write your love letter.

After you answer all the questions above and maybe some of your own, let your journal sit for a couple of days. You may find you forgot something and want to add to it. A memory of you and your dog walking on the beach, climbing a mountain, or sleeping all cuddled up in bed might come back to you that you had forgotten.

Keep in mind though that this letter doesn't have to be perfect. Your dog doesn't mind that you spelled something wrong or that your sentence isn't complete. Your dog is just happy to know that you are with him or her on this journey because it can be stressful for him or her as well.

The more that you can give back to your dog at his or her end-of-life period, the better you are going to feel after your dog has died. Even if you only have a week after the diagnosis to deal with your grief, whatever you can do will help you.

At the same time, please keep in mind that this exercise is not time-sensitive. If you are a person that only has moments left before your dog dies, writing a love letter after he or she dies is extremely helpful with processing your grief.

Step 2 — The Love Letter

After you feel like you have everything down that you want to tell your dog, it is now time to take out a fresh piece of paper or open a new word document and write your love letter.

The first thing to do is put the date on the top of your letter. The reason for this is that sometime in the future, whether months or years from now, you will probably come across your letter. It will help you put in perspective where you were in your coping with your pet loss journey and how far you have come.

You might even want this letter as a eulogy for your dog's funeral if you choose to mourn your loss in this manner. We will cover pet funerals in detail in the second book of *The Pet Bereavement Series: My Dog Has Died: What Do I Do?*

Then start your letter with "Dear [name of your dog]." I suggest beginning the letter with your dog's name rather than a nickname. You can always include the nicknames in the body of the letter, but using his or her given name allows you to have a conversation that is equal and respectful.

Then start telling your dog all those things that you brainstormed in your list, all those responses to the essential questions. If you find it is difficult to write just one letter, then do as many as you want.

The time that you spend on your letter is up to you. Some of my clients spend a little time each day writing. Some will write the entire letter in one sitting. No matter how you choose to write it, be sure to get the letter done. You will be so happy that you did.

Step 3 — Delivery

Then after your letter is written, go with your dog to a special place where you both are comfortable. I suggest you do this alone with your dog. That way you can give your dog full attention without worrying about others.

Your dog loves you, and you love your dog. Cherish that and write him or her a love letter. Cuddle with your dog while you read it out loud and feel good about how you are walking this journey of pet loss grief.

The end-of-the-chapter *Contemplation Questions* will give you more direction in the writing and delivering of your love letter to your beloved pet.

Chapter Wrap-Up

In this chapter we talked about how writing a love letter helps you to feel deeper love and connection with your dog. Plus it helps in the self-support of your feelings of pet grief. I gave you the essential questions and other important aspects to consider when writing and delivering the love letter to your dog.

Please use the chapter's *Contemplation Questions* to further guide you through the process of writing and reading your love letter to your dog.

In the next chapter you will get information on what you can expect after your dog reaches the end of his or her life. You will learn how to plan for ways in which your life will be different and how to cope with these changes.

Chapter Thirteen Contemplation Questions

1. I shared with you some essential questions from my Rescue Joy from Pet Loss Grief Program that help in laying the groundwork for writing your love letter. Is there anything that you can add that you want to tell your dog?

2. Do you have any feelings of pet grief while you write or when you read this letter to your dog?

3. What are you going to pay most attention to during this special time that you have with your dog?

14. What to Expect after Death

I totally understand that you are very sad and the last thing you want to think about is what to expect after your dog dies—while your dog is still living his or her last days, weeks, or months. I understand, and I am sad that you are going through what you are. Even still, know that my goal is to continue to help you through this difficult time.

As with all the other places I've described to you on your grief journey, it is essential that you prepare yourself for what is to come—whether that be the common and incorrect myths (chapter 2), the seven stages of grief (chapter 3), the insensitive comments from friends or family (chapter 5), determining when the time is right for the final day (chapter 12), and now—what to expect after the death of your dog. I want to give you as many tools as I can so that you feel supported throughout your journey and know what to expect.

Anticipation and preparation are so important to ensure your grief journey is one that includes grace and compassion along with the other common, but uncomfortable, feelings that come with loss.

Case Study — Julie and Sparky

Julie found that by knowing what she was going to experience after Sparky's death, she was able to navigate the challenges better. By knowing what to expect, she could deal with the multitude of changes in her life with more clarity and strength.

Julie shared—

> *At first I thought it was crazy to talk about what would be different in my life after Sparky died, but now I see that planning ahead as much as possible is a healthy experience. Yes, I still dreaded the day when I had to make my decision to end Sparky's life, and I grieve his death every single day of my life; however, if I didn't know what to expect, I would not be able to function with my feelings of grief. I am so thankful I took the time to understand what was going to happen to me.*

Julie's experience helped her understand how important it was to know what to expect. It helped her remember that her grief journey was unique to her and it was also normal. With this knowledge she was able to proceed as she wished with her grief journey.

Possible Experiences

Here are some of unexpected things that Julie experienced that you may or may not experience after your dog dies.

You may become aware of the . . .

- different and unexpected changes in your life
- time where you really felt the full extent of your loss
- ways to redefine your relationship with your deceased dog

- new discoveries of some areas of personal growth through your pet grief

- joyful memories that you shared together

Remember this can be a very challenging time period for you. You will feel both the extent of your loss as well as the emergence of new feelings of grief. During this stretch of time, you will begin to recognize how your life is changing.

You are experiencing and learning who you are without your dog. You may move into a phase of discovering and understanding life without the physical presence of your dog.

You may spend time with new friends, have different adventures, or do things you have always wanted to do but never did.

You may begin to think about getting another dog or volunteering at your local humane society.

You may even have some feelings of relief, which is perfectly normal to feel. If your dog was very ill and suffered a lot during the end of his or her life, you may feel relieved that your dog has reached the end of life and is no longer suffering. This too is a normal feeling to have.

There are many things that will happen during this stage of pet loss grief, and they will be unique to you.

Please use the three *Contemplation Questions* at the end of the chapter to help you be prepared for these changes and to establish the action that you can take to heal your pet grief.

Beautiful and Forever

There is no prescribed timeframe when you will experience these feelings or even have these feelings at all. The relationship that you had with your dog is special to the both of you. And that will never change.

Your dog will live in your heart forever. This is a beautiful blessing that is private and special to the both of you. Those special moments on the beach, cuddled on the couch, and the love that you shared will never go away. Yet your active grief will change over the days, weeks, months, and years after your dog dies, and something new will begin to develop.

The Metamorphosis of Grief

Another feeling that you may begin to recognize is more joy in your life. Please rest assured—it doesn't mean that you will no longer experience grief from the loss of your dog. It just means that you will begin to feel a shift in your awareness in regard to your grief in a different way. We will discuss this more in the next chapter.

When you are experiencing these changes in your life, you will be able to continue to acknowledge and honor your grief. Expect that your feelings of grief will resurface. Remember that is normal. But, you will be able to recognize and celebrate your growth and gains during this time as well!

No matter what your experience is during this time, continue to believe in your own process. Your grief is unique to you! It will continue to change, so it is important to reflect upon what you are going through.

Chapter Wrap-Up

As with the other parts of your grief journey, even after your dog passes it is important to establish expectations and anticipate what your life may be like. In doing this, you are preparing yourself, which in turn helps you navigate your grief journey and the time after your dog passes with more grace, compassion, and grounding.

After your dog dies, you will begin to recognize some changes in your life that may seem out of place. And certain parts of your grief process will remain constant even though others will change.

In the next chapter, we explore happiness. I will show you that choosing happiness is part of the normal grieving process. You will learn that choosing happiness will not take away the forever bond that you share with your dog. You will learn about your "new normal."

Chapter Fourteen Contemplation Questions

1. You learned the ways in which you can expect changes in your life after your dog reaches the end of life. Are there any expected changes that you anticipate you will experience?

2. Do you have any feelings of pet grief with recognizing these changes?

3. With the changes that you expect for yourself after your dog dies, what are the ways in which you can prepare yourself to feel supported?

15. Choosing Happiness

You might be thinking right now, while your dog is terminally ill, that it is simply wrong or impossible for you to contemplate feeling future joy or happiness. In fact you may even think it is ridiculous to even consider. Maybe you are asking why I am even bringing it up.

For now, please consider that this is something for you to be prepared for. Even though you are feeling intense grief right now, there will be a time when you will get to feel joy and happiness again.

Joy may be the last thing on your mind, and that is okay. As with other steps in your grief journey, anticipating and preparing for what is to come is essential, so that's why we need to map out this step, the step of choosing happiness.

Section Three Quick Recap

Throughout this final section of *My Dog is Dying: What Do I Do?*, you explored some very difficult and challenging issues that you may or may not be ready for. Awareness of these things is a crucial element of your successful navigation of the pet loss journey.

In this third section you have been given tools for coping with your dog's illness. Section 3 has offered you ways to prepare as best you can for your dog's last day in his or her cycle of life, tools that can give you calmness and clearheadedness amidst the chaos. Plus we addressed how preparing for the making of tough decisions early on can help you gain even greater connection to the love that you feel for your dog.

You wrote a beautiful love letter to your dog, thanking him or her for the life that you both shared. This letter is another way in which you can tell your dog how much you love and appreciate him or her.

In the previous chapter, I helped you with some changes you may undergo when your dog reaches the end of life. We talked about how you will begin to recognize changes in yourself that may seem out of place. We also talked about how certain parts of your grief process will remain constant even though other parts will change.

Now I am going to share with you even more supportive tools that will guide you on how to rescue your joy after your dog dies.

Preparing for Your "New Normal"

Even though your dog has not reached the end of life, it is important to be aware of the changes that will eventually occur, changes around you and within you.

Keep in mind that during this time period, expectations are going to increase from the people around you. This will be the time when you will begin to live your life differently than before, and some people may not understand that.

This period does take time to adjust to, and we touched on it some in the previous chapter. I referred to it as your "new normal." In your "new normal," please be aware that you may experience both feelings of relief and possibly joy, both of which you may not have anticipated you'd feel. Because feeling relief and joy at this stage on your journey of grief can be unexpected and possibly even unsettling, I want to offer you guidance, so you can move through this "new normal" with grace and compassion for yourself.

Even though your dog has not reached the end of life yet, being prepared for these feelings and how people are going to react to you is important.

Here is how a "new normal" can be described.

When you lose something in your life, whether it be a spouse, family member, dog, limb, etc., that loss creates a completely different way for you to live your daily life. In this case, when your dog is no longer there for you to depend on or for him or her to depend on you, it will be a difficult period of time because that void challenges you to develop a new identity for yourself—and more.

Case Study — Patty and Nila

Patty was part of my Rescue Joy from Pet Loss Grief support program. Patty and I talked a lot about how to cope with life after a pet dies and her "new normal."

Patty had a rough time with the death of Nila. Nila had been her constant companion. They did everything together. She went to work with Patty every single day and was part of Patty's physical therapy practice.

When Nila died, Patty's world completely changed. She lost her best friend, work partner, and confidant. Patty felt that she would never be able to be happy again.

Patty confided—

> *Without Nila in my life, I cannot feel any joy or happiness. That would be disrespectful to Nila. I don't know who I am. My friends don't understand my sadness, and I don't know what I am going to do or who I am without Nila. I just want her back in my life, and everything will be perfect, and I will be happy.*

Here is the thing about what Patty was experiencing—everything that she said is considered *normal grief*. She was experiencing a very huge loss in her life. For her to be able to express what she did was very healthy.

Five Steps for Discovering Your "New Normal"

When Patty was ready, I shared with her the following five steps for discovering her "new normal." Hopefully they will help you as well with what you are experiencing.

1. A New Identity

While your dog is ill and you are preparing for the end of his or her life, your normal routines change. You are not the same person, and your normal activities with your dog are shifting and may even be gone.

Then when your dog has died, you no longer have a physical relationship with your dog. And you may never be the same as you were before your dog died.

Your self-identity will naturally change when your dog is ill and when he or she dies. Patty experienced this when she noticed people saying to her, "I remember you—you are Nila's mom" or "You are that awesome person that used to hike this mountain with your dog."

This is all part of your grief journey and something to keep in mind when planning out how you are going to create your new life. We will cover this more in *Book 2: My Dog Has Died*.

2. A New Relationship with Your Dog That Died

Many of my clients that are in my Rescue Joy From Pet Loss Grief program work on a common goal—to not forget their dog but to change the relationship from a physical presence to one of wonderful memories or a spiritual relationship.

The checklist that you created in chapter 2 will help you stay on task so that you can spend quality time with your dog rather than always worrying that you didn't do enough or forgot to do something in regards to his or her care.

In your Reminiscence List from chapter 7 and with the template to create your own list that you downloaded in chapter 2, you will have many memories that will help you build a new relationship with your dog.

This list will include what you did together, funny antics of your dog, and maybe even some things that you learned from your dog. These memories are treasures, and no one can take them away.

Plus in chapter 13 you had a beautiful experience of writing a love letter to your dog, thanking your pet for all the wonderful things that he or she gave you.

By forming your new identity without your dog and allowing yourself to enjoy memories, you will begin to have a new relationship with your dog based on a different type of connection.

In *Book 2: My Dog Has Died* and *Book 3: My Dog Is Gone* we will talk more about creating a spiritual or nonphysical relationship with your dog so that you can continue to have a different type of bond with your beloved pet.

3. A New Group of Friends

Many people don't understand or respect the fact that losing a dog is painful. You may find that searching for new friends that are more supportive of you is important. For example, you may end up relying on and investing more time into the relationships with the people who were most supportive and nonjudgmental of you in your grief journey.

Also, if you were involved with any dog groups or obedience classes, you developed friendships that included dogs. Not having a dog right now can change the relationship that you have with these people. You may feel left out or have the feeling that you can no longer relate to them.

4. A New Sense of Purpose

It is normal to question your purpose in life once your dog dies. Your dog made a difference in your life and depended on you. Now that your dog has died, you may be questioning the meaning of your current existence. This is normal.

Some people realize new life purposes and make significant life changes after their dogs have died. For example, some decide to volunteer at their local humane societies, start dog rescue groups of their own, or start helping others with pet loss grief.

5. Celebration of Your Growth

When your dog dies, your journey of pet loss grief is life-altering. You didn't choose to experience the loss of your pet. Grief is usually unwanted or unplanned. However, the journey of grief is a wonderful experience for personal growth. Celebrate how you have grown from the opportunity to share life with your pet. Find joy with your growth and the lessons learned.

Some people learn through this experience how to be more sensitive to others going through the loss of their dogs. Some decide to give back to dogs in need. Some learn to celebrate the gifts that their dogs gave them and live their lives fully with that in mind.

After Patty worked through these five steps and discovered a different way of dealing with her grief, she was able to then celebrate her life with Nila. She began to feel okay that she was starting to feel joy and happiness again.

Did her grief go away? No, it did not, but it changed.

Patty shared with me at the end of the Rescue Joy from Pet Loss Grief program—

> *I never thought it would be possible to be happy again without Nila in my life. I thought that feeling happy would be disrespectful to Nila. By exploring the five steps that you gave me, I was able to discover what I was feeling was normal. I could still have feelings of happiness and joy amongst my grief.*

Even though you never forget your loss, you can learn different ways to live your life without your dog being physically with you.

Understanding that grief works in different ways can help you have an enriching experience and support your "new normal" as well. Please note that I will be offering even more ways to support your "new normal" in detail in the second book in *The Pet Bereavement Series* called *My Dog Has Died: What Do I Do?*

Know that having an understanding of what happens to you after your dog dies will prepare you for the unexpected. Knowing what to expect and planning for it will help you rescue your joy and not feel like it is a horrible feeling to have.

Having to say good-bye to your beloved dog is difficult. After all, he or she is your family and your best friend.

Your dog is here for only a short time compared to you, and the loss of a dog often brings up many feelings that are sometimes really difficult to deal with. That's why guidance, support, and preparation are so crucial to your successful navigation of the pet grief journey. That's why you've sought out *My Dog Is Dying: What Do I Do?*

Chapter Wrap-Up

Choosing happiness is part of the normal grieving process. Choosing happiness will not take away the forever bond that you share with your dog.

Please revisit the five steps for discovering your "new normal" to assist you in dealing with the fact that your dog is no longer physically with you.

Your journey with pet grief is unique to you and your dog. Honor your journey with respect and dignity for yourself and your companion. No one can alter that if you are aware of and accountable for your process.

Keep in mind that your dog gave you unending unconditional love. Now is your time to give that gift back to your dog. Allow yourself to feel the joy that your dog gave you.

Here are your last three *Contemplation Questions* that will help you rescue your joy from pet loss grief. Dedicate yourself to these questions only when you are ready.

Chapter Fifteen Contemplation Questions

1. What ways has your dog shown you happiness in life?

2. What feelings of grief are you experiencing as you write down your feelings of joy and happiness?

3. Now that you understand that feeling joy and happiness is normal, can you list some of the ways in which you may be experiencing these feelings?

Conclusion

Your dog plays an essential role in your life. You share adventures, emotions, and passions. Together you give each other a multitude of gifts that in some way make both of your lives a little easier and a lot more fun.

Your dog connects you to nature, other people, other animals, and new ways of looking at life. He or she provides you with emotional nourishment that can be difficult to get from people. Plus your furry companion is your everyday personal trainer that keeps you healthy by never giving up on telling you that it is time for a walk!

Your dog teaches you about the joys in life and why choosing happiness is a better option than getting caught up with things that don't matter. In other words, he or she makes you laugh, plays, and encourages you to take things a bit less seriously.

Your pet companion provides you with daily physical contact and comfort that is unique and personal.

Your dog conscientiously joins you when you experience the greatest adventures of your life and continues to do so even with the most mundane of tasks without complaint.

Your dog listens to your secrets that no other person may even know. It is private and confidential, something that only the two of you completely understand.

It is, therefore, no surprise then that when you get the news that your dog is dying that it creates some level of grief. This is huge and horrible news, and when something this significant is taken from your life, your entire world can change.

You can expect that you are going to feel sad, lonely, angry, hungry, not hungry, disoriented, and all the other normal feelings of grief.

Since your relationship with your dog is completely unique from that with anyone else, expect that your experience with pet loss grief is unique to you and your dog too. It all depends on your personality, your dog's personality, and your life experiences. What you experience will be completely different than that of someone else.

You are also going to experience that some people are just not going to get what you are going through. That is okay. It is not your job to change their opinions.

The important thing to do is to honor your dog, which you learned to do in this book and will learn more about in *Book 2: My Dog Has Died: What Do I Do? Grief, Joy, and Celebrations for Healing*. And by all means, honor and trust yourself and the grief journey that you are walking. Surround yourself with friends, support groups, and a pet loss coach that will offer you support without judgment.

Remember to take care of yourself physically. If you are tired and feeling exhausted, you will not be able to be present for your dog and what he or she is experiencing. You are the caretaker now, and by taking care of yourself, you will be able to give your dog the quality time that he or she deserves.

By planning ahead and anticipating things on your journey, you can be more present and loving for your dog and in turn experience more grace and compassion on this difficult and painful journey.

Yet, your grief journey will not end when your dog dies. That is normal.

Book 2 in The Pet Bereavement Series

In the next book, entitled *My Dog Has Died: What Do I Do? Grief, Joy, and Celebrations for Healing*, you will learn ways to continue to walk your journey of pet loss grief with kindness and consideration for yourself.

There will be a lot of changes in your life, and at times during this stage of your journey, you are going to feel incredibly alone. Your dog is no longer physically in your life, and that is a big deal.

Book 2 is going to take you by the hand and support you with tools and options on how you can walk this part of your pet loss journey.

Here is an example of just a few of the many topics that you will be able to explore.

Discover how your grief will be similar yet somewhat different after your dog dies.

People are going to react differently to you and say some things to you that don't feel good. You are going to get information and help on how you can protect your grieving heart.

1. Celebrate your dog by learning ways to create a special pet memorial, pet funeral, or celebration of life ceremony.

   Your dog was not just a pet. Your dog was your best friend and family member. Not only will the second book present options and decisions for taking care of your dog's body (cremations, green burial, etc.), but it helps you discover how healthy it is to process your grief by creating a beautiful pet memorial service or pet funeral.

2. Discover ways to rescue your joy from pet loss grief by exploring new ways to live your life that still continue to honor your dog.

When you enjoy the memories that you shared with your dog, it will help you experience your grief in a healthy way. We will explore how not to forget about your dog after he or she dies and the most appropriate length of your grieving period for your dog. Plus, you will know when the time is right to get a new dog and be able to make other important decisions as well.

Resources

Center for Pet Loss Grief
Through Life, Death, **and** *Beyond*

Wendy Van de Poll, MS, CEOL

https://centerforpetlossgrief.com

Best Selling and Award Winning Books
https://centerforpetlossgrief.com/books

My Dog IS Dying: What Do I Do?
My Dog HAS Died: What Do I Do?

My Cat IS Dying: What Do I Do?
My Cat HAS Died: What Do I Do?

Healing A Child's Pet Loss Grief

Free Book
Healing Your Heart From Pet Loss Grief

Free Pet Grief Support Kit
https://centerforpetlossgrief.com

Animal Mediumship
https://centerforpetlossgrief.com/animal-medium

Animal Communication
https://wendyvandepoll.com/animal-communication

Pet Funerals
https://centerforpetlossgrief.com/pet-funeral

Facebook
Center for Pet Loss Grief
https://facebook.com/centerforpetlossgrief

Pet Memorial Support Group
https://facebook.com/groups/petmemorials.
centerforpetlossgrief

Other Resources

Holistic Veterinarians: American Holistic Veterinary Medical Association
www.ahvma.org

Online Herbal Support: Pet Wellness Blends
www.herbs-for-life-3.myshopify.com/#_l_1e

Magnetic Therapy Supplies: aVivoPur
www.bit.ly/2Op6XHk

Support Groups: Association for Pet Loss and Bereavement
www.aplb.org

International Association for Animal Hospice and Palliative Care
www.iaahpc.org

Association of Human-Animal Bond Veterinarians
www.ahabv.org

Book 2 in The Pet Bereavement Series

My Dog Has Died: What Do I Do?
Making Decisions and Healing the Trauma of Pet Loss

More pet grief support—Your pet was your best friend! Care for YOUR heart during a tough time!

Are you feeling alone with the loss of your pet? Are people's eyes glazing over when you express your grief? Are family, friends, and coworkers telling you to move on because it was only a dog? Are you worried that your grief is not normal?

First of all, let me assure you that GRIEF IS NORMAL! After such a devastating loss, it is perfectly healthy to feel sad, angry, disoriented, depressed, etc. And it is not weird or silly to seek out pet grief support. These feelings are just part of the necessary grieving stages to go through.

I know these feelings very well as I have been there with my own dogs, and with each one I learned something really beautiful and joyful in my life. That is why I created a way to walk the journey of pet grief support with you.

I do GET GRIEF, and in my experience I have found that . . .

1. As humans, we all experience grief, and we can't avoid it. It is part of life.

2. It is healthy to express our grief rather than stuff it in. Stuffing it in only makes it worse. IT TAKES WORK!

3. It is extremely important to find a supportive friend, group, or end-of-life coach that will provide a SAFE place for you to express your grief. Not many people are comfortable with the grieving process, so choose wisely.

Your grieving process after the death of your dog is delicate, unique, and extremely important. When your beloved companion dies, this second book will support you through the final stages of grief and the mourning period as well. It can be an extremely difficult time—your life suddenly is not normal anymore because you lost your pet. It can take time to find a new normal.

This second book can help you with your grieving heart. Are you asking yourself some of these following questions now that your dog has died?

- Am I normal to feel such intense sadness, anger like I do?

- Why does everyone tell me I should move on?

- How long will I grieve for my pet loss, and what are the grieving stages?

- How can I not forget about my pet after he or she dies?

- How is grief normal?

- What ways can I grieve that are healthy?

- When is the right time to get a new pet?

- Am I ready to actively work on my feelings of grief?

My Dog Has Died: What Do I Do? will help you heal your pet loss grief.

Your pet was your best friend! Care for YOUR heart during a tough time!

Acknowledgments

I would like to thank my clients who felt safe to express their grief stories with me so that I could write this book to help others.

To all the fur, feather, and fin gurus who taught me those imperative life lessons that as humans we sometimes would like to avoid.

I am truly appreciative of the work done by my editor, Nancy Pile, who added her heart and paws to improve the book for your reading enjoyment. And to my meticulous and amazing formatter Debbie Lum.

A huge hug goes to my husband, Rick. His inspiration and support was and still is over-the-top amazing.

About the Author

Wendy Van de Poll is a pioneering leader in the field of pet loss grief support. Wendy is dedicated to providing a safe place for her clients to express their grief over the loss of their pets.

What makes Wendy successful with her clients is that she get's grief! *"Over the years I've dealt with my own grief and helping many families communicate and connect with their pets long after their loss. It's what I've done since I was just 5 yrs old!"*

She is compassionate and supportive to all who know her.

Her passion is to help people when they are grieving over the loss of a pet and her larger than life love for animals has led her to devote her life to the mission of increasing the quality of life between animals and people no matter what stage they are in their cycle of life! She has been called the animal whisperer.

She is a Certified End of Life and Pet Grief Support Coach, Certified Pet Funeral Celebrant, Animal Medium and Communicator and Licensed Massage Therapist for Human, Horse and Hound. She is the founder of The Center for Pet Loss Grief and an international best selling and award-winning author and speaker.

She holds a Master's of Science degree in Wolf Ecology and Behavior and has run with wild wolves in Minnesota, coyotes in Massachusetts and foxes in her backyard. She lives in the woods with her husband, two crazy birds, her rescue dog Addie and all kinds of wildlife.

Wendy currently has a Skype, phone, and in-person practice, providing end-of-life and pet grief support coaching, animal communication and mediumship, and personalized pet funerals.

You can reach her at www.centerpetlossgrief.com or www.wendyvandepoll.com

Thank You for Reading

My Dog Is Dying: What Do I Do?

Emotions, Decisions, and Options for Healing

Hi, my name is Marley or the Divine Ms. M. Since this book is dedicated to me, it would mean a lot if you left a review on Amazon.

I died on September 25, 2014 of cancer, and I remember my mom saying when she heard the news I was going to die—"What am I going to do without Marley in my life?"

My goal is to help everyone around me to choose happiness in their lives no matter what.

I loved that my mom wrote this book to help you on your pet loss journey. I would be grateful if you would leave a helpful REVIEW on Amazon: **http://a.co/0KaS1gn**

Thank you,

Marley Van de Poll

The Pet Bereavement Series

Best Selling and Award Winning Books

By Wendy Van de Poll, MS, CEOL

My Dog IS Dying: What Do I Do?
My Dog HAS Died: What Do I Do?

My Cat IS Dying: What Do I Do?
My Cat HAS Died: What Do I Do?

Healing A Child's Pet Loss Grief

Free Book

Healing Your Heart From Pet Loss Grief

Printed in the USA
CPSIA information can be obtained
at www.ICGtesting.com
LVHW090908061123
763094LV00036B/210